"Developing and implementing an effective performance management system remains a challenge for many public health organizations. Thanks to Jack, Sonja, and Amanda, they have made performance management less daunting and produced a guide to help organizations more effectively manage performance. Their experience is evident, and the guidance they provide clear and concise."

Ron Bialek, *President of the Public Health Foundation, USA*

"*Collaborative Performance Management for Public Health: A Practical Guide* is a must-read for public health departments. At a time when performance management is essential to ensuring accountability, this book provides the info public health practitioners need to incorporate PM into their daily work. Kudos to the authors for an outstanding, practical resource!"

Kaye Bender, *RN, FAAN, Public Health Accreditation Board, USA*

Collaborative Performance Management for Public Health

Performance management can be an uncomfortable topic within the discipline of public health. Written by leaders in public health performance management and quality improvement, this book carefully explains what public health performance management is – and makes a strong case for why it is needed to tackle successfully the long-standing health issues plaguing communities and states. Notably, the book eschews the need to invest in technology or to learn a new performance management vocabulary. Rather the authors advocate for more thoughtful use of the resources already available in the organization, relying on public health leadership working in conjunction with well trained staff to manage their own organizational performance.

To be broadly accepted within public health, performance management concepts and models have to be framed and populated with public health examples, and this book offers a wealth of practical insights and case studies that may be immediately applied to public health organizations, from assessing an organization's needs, introducing a performance management system to the organization, developing an agency's goals and targets, to implementation of sound performance management systems and plans. *Collaborative Performance Management for Public Health* is required reading for all public health leaders and employees concerned with maximizing the health impact of scarce resources.

Amanda E. McCarty is an Assistant Professor in Health Services Administration at West Virginia University Institute of Technology. Previously, she served as the Director of Performance Management and Systems Development at the West Virginia's Bureau for Public Health. As a consultant for the Public Health Foundation, McCarty has provided training and technical assistance for state, local and tribal health departments in the areas of performance management systems development, workforce development, quality improvement, and the development of evaluation plans and logic models since 2013.

Sonja M. Armbruster is on the faculty of Wichita State University's Public Health Sciences program, and recently served as Director of the Center for Public Health Initiatives at Wichita State University's Community Engagement Institute. She previously served as adjunct faculty for the University of Kansas Master of Public Health program. As a consultant for the Public Health Foundation she provides training and technical assistance for state, local and tribal health departments in the areas of performance management systems development, workforce development, quality improvement since 2011.

John W. Moran is a Senior Quality Advisor to the Public Health Foundation and an Adjunct Professor in the Arizona State University College of Health Solutions' School for the Science of Health Care Delivery. He has more than 30 years of expertise in developing quality improvement tools and training programs, implementing and evaluating quality improvement programs, and writing books and articles on quality improvement methods. His past appointments include Senior Fellow at the University of Minnesota, School of Public Health in the Division of Health Policy and Management; President of the Advisory Board of Choose To Be Healthy Coalition of the Healthy Maine Partnership for York County, Maine; faculty member of the CDC/IHI Antibiotic Stewardship project; PHAB's Evaluation and Quality Improvement Committee; and more than 20 years as an Adjunct Professor in the Graduate and Undergraduate School of Engineering at the University of Lowell.

Collaborative Performance Management for Public Health

A Practical Guide

Amanda E. McCarty, Sonja M. Armbruster and John W. Moran

NEW YORK AND LONDON

First published 2020
by Routledge
52 Vanderbilt Avenue, New York, NY 10017

and by Routledge
2 Park Square, Milton Park, Abingdon, Oxon, OX14 4RN

Routledge is an imprint of the Taylor & Francis Group, an informa business

Library of Congress Cataloging-in-Publication Data
A catalog record for this title has been requested

ISBN: 978-0-367-51526-3 (hbk)
ISBN: 978-1-003-05449-8 (ebk)

Typeset in Times New Roman
by Wearset Ltd, Boldon, Tyne and Wear

Contents

Tables

Figures

Foreword

Collaborative Performance Management for Public Health – A Practical Guide

Mythology abounds surrounding the concepts of performance management (PM) within the discipline of public health. Often when the topic arises, people of sound minds ordinarily well-grounded in public health principles and practice, staunch advocates for evidence based public health, become visibly uncomfortable. The ensuing conversation lacks vestiges of common sense, as all reason exits the room as if hermetically sealed. Worse, logic and deep thought are banished from entry. Hence the need for this book, penned by leaders in public health PM and quality improvement (QI). The authors go to great pains to clarify what public health PM is – and is not. Moreover, they make a strong case for why it is needed for our shared discipline if we are to tackle successfully the long-standing health issues plaguing our communities and states.

Sometimes public health struggles to adopt new principles widely accepted in other enterprises. PM and QI are prime examples, routinely incorporated into almost all other areas of commerce, even as government (not solely public health) lag behind. Having been part of the early introduction of these important tools and frameworks, I now have a better sense of the challenge. To be broadly accepted within public health, the concepts and models have to be framed and populated with public health examples. In *A Practical Guide to Comprehensive Performance Management in Public Health* that is precisely what the authors strive to do – to make their strongest case in terms that public health practitioners can closely identify with. And they have done so brilliantly.

I recommend reading this book. It compels deeper thinking on the part of the reader regarding the PM model you may already have in place. Yet it does this without urging deeper investment in technology or the need to learn a new PM vocabulary. Rather it advocates for more thoughtful use of the resources at hand, and profound confidence that leadership working in conjunction with well trained staff can achieve the desired synergy by truly managing organizational performance.

Often, implementing PM is not easy. Moreover, it is not for the faint of heart or the timid. It is for leaders who genuinely are attracted to leadership roles, who seek to maximize the health impact of the scarce resources the public has entrusted with our agencies. If that is what motivates you, read this book and learn from the straightforward lessons of your experienced colleagues in *A Practical Guide to Comprehensive Performance Management in Public Health.*

Leslie M. Beitsch, MD, JD
Chair, Dept. of Behavioral Sciences and Social Medicine
Center for Medicine and Public Health
Florida State University College of Medicine

1 Performance Management in Public Health

Performance Management (PM) is a systematic process which helps an organization achieve its mission and strategic goals by improving effectiveness, empowering employees, and streamlining decision making.[1] Public Health departments have been encouraged by accreditation standards, funding initiatives and funding accountability efforts to develop several agency plans that represent their capacity to meet the essential public health services through workforce structure, program performance and outcomes, plans for improvement, and their priority areas of focus for the near future. It is also beneficial to have regular monitoring of progress, collect data that helps guide decision making and rely on that information to determine if efforts are successful and making an impact. In the case of public health, the ultimate purpose of these efforts is to improve the public's health.[2]

Performance Management goes hand-in-hand with the concepts of quality improvement (QI) and accountability. Based on recent public health agency reports and literature, PM practices have measurably improved public health outputs and outcomes, created efficiencies working with partners, and helped staff and management teams solve problems.[2] By establishing standards, setting goals, collecting data to ensure accountability, PM helps agencies demonstrate value and impact. When applied across the agency in a "system-wide" effort, data are being collected on a regular basis to monitor and improve performance across all functions. This includes public health programs, human resources, budget planning, customer satisfaction, workforce development, strategic planning, etc. Given resource needs and areas of focus for each, it can often be difficult for agency-wide activities and plans (health improvement plan, strategic plan, workforce development plan, etc.) to work in collaboration with one another, versus existing as separate silos within the agency. The Performance Management System (PM System) is the centralized component of these public health agency efforts and plans working together. Figure A.1 in the Appendix of this book includes a *PHAB Plan Alignment Crosswalk* that seeks to offer clarity about the interconnected nature of these plans and the power of the PM System to unify the work.

Foundations in Performance Management

Performance Management is not new to the governmental public health system of state, local, tribal and territorial health departments. Established in 2000, the Turning Point Performance Management National Excellence Collaborative (PMC) – a four-year project funded by The Robert Wood Johnson Foundation – aspired to "move the field of public health from simply measuring performance of individual programs to actively measuring and managing the performance of an entire agency or 'system'."[2] That work laid the foundation for the way public health PM is defined and practiced. That series of reports is referenced in this chapter and elsewhere in the book, available online, and still worthy of review. The Turning Point work defined the four quadrants of public health PM referenced in the Public Health Accreditation Board Standards and Measures.[5] While these were published in 2013, the work to develop this guidance began in 2007, when the Public Health Accreditation Board was formed. The Standards and Measures guide best practices for health departments, whether or not they seek accreditation. Related to PM, the guidance requires leadership and staff engagement including training, a system/policy, agency assessment and a team. All of these elements are addressed in this book and mentioned here as evidence that a functioning PM System is fundamental to agency success. One barrier to progress when developing PM Systems is push-back from staff; and one source of staff frustration is the constantly changing landscape of models and innovations and new frameworks. PM can feel the same when introduced or re-energized within agencies. Some barriers can be overcome with the recognition that this work is not just the new and urgent idea of the day, but instead foundational, consistent and results-oriented.

First Steps

Seek First to Understand

Before building or improving a PM System, it is important to understand what is already in place and working effectively within the agency. Seeking first to understand the system that exists is wise as it honors the work being done while beginning to identify potential champions and barriers to the process. Review the landscape and determine which programs or divisions that have established (documented) goals or standards. If so, are data being used to establish these goals and standards? Is quality improvement a regular part of improving processes and programs? Components of a PM system may already be in place and could be working really well in some areas. Begin by meeting with each program or office director within the agency and discuss what they have in place. A questionnaire can be developed to ensure consistent information is being gathered from each program. Questions can include:

- Does the program have established goals or standards to be achieved each year?
- If yes:
    - How are those established?
    - Gather examples
- Does the program collect data and use that information to guide decisions or change the way programs/services are being offered?
- If yes:
    - Are measures monitored on a regular basis throughout the year?
    - How are those measures determined?
    - What is the reporting mechanism?
    - If the information gathered is not as expected, are QI efforts being implemented to improve processes?
    - Who is this information being shared with and for what purpose?
    - Gather examples

Collecting this information for each program throughout the agency will provide a good understanding of what is currently in place, where strengths related to PM and QI exist throughout, and identify areas where these efforts will be new. This exercise will also help to identify any best practices that may exist that could easily be built upon to assist other programs. It will also shed light on those who have experience with PM and QI and who may be great resources to lean on throughout this process. If available, they would also be great candidates for implementation and support teams. Design teams, support teams, and PM/QI Councils will be discussed later in the book.

Self-Assessment

Understanding strengths and opportunities for improvement related to PM and QI throughout the agency is also a good place to start. The Performance Management Self-Assessment developed by the Public Health Foundation prompts agencies and programs to identify strengths and areas for improvement.[3] Designed to be completed by a team of colleagues (not in an individual setting), the assessment generates group discussions around the components of a PM system. Whether the agency has a robust system or is just starting to consider PM, the PM Self-Assessment can help the team determine if it has the structure in place to support achieving objectives and continually improving performance.[3]

The five parts of the Performance Management Self-Assessment include the following, and will all be discussed in later detail throughout the book:

- Visible Leadership
- Performance Standards
- Performance Measurement
- Reporting Progress
- Quality Improvement

Collaborative PM efforts should be driven by community or customer priorities, which should then drive agency priorities, programmatic goals and objectives. What exactly does that mean? How is the agency determining priorities? Agencies vary in methods used to determine priorities and can include:

- Governing body priorities
- Previous year budgeting priorities
- Funding streams and Grants
- "What we've always done"
- Media focus

None of these answers are wrong per se, but they are not necessarily based on the needs of the community or the customer. Yes, the customer: the members of the community served are the customer. Without the community, the public health agency would no longer exist. To some degree, most health departments offer a standard set of services and programs and then beyond that, most health departments are unique in offering additional services. But without the people using programs and services, the agency would not be here. Including the customer in PM planning efforts will be a central theme throughout.

Training

Training is another foundational first – and continuous – step to assuring success with PM System development and implementation. Providing support that builds the capacity of the workforce is fundamental to the success of this endeavor. In an article titled. "Building Collective Efficacy to Support Public Health Workforce Development," the authors explain that "a strategic adult learning approach can improve both individual capabilities and the collective performance of the workforce."[7] This is particularly true for PM System development training. Staff need skills, but they also need time to collectively learn together and as the authors state from their study, this builds "the collective belief of workers in the ability of the group to succeed."[7]

Urgency for Performance Management System Development

Improvement is needed in Public Health Performance Management Work

In the article, "Achieving *Public Health* Standards and Increasing Accreditation Readiness," the authors assessed accreditation readiness among 67 public health agencies who had received funds to support accreditation readiness work through the National Public Health Improvement Initiative. Among all PHAB standards, "The standards with the most gaps reported were standard 9.1 (use a performance management system to monitor achievement of organizational objectives), standard."[8] Despite the foundations of Public Health Performance Management dating back to 2000 and sooner, this work continues to need support, focus and infrastructure. The resources, steps, processes and strategies that follow in this book are intended to help close this gap.

A Tool for Story-Telling

The PM System is the centralized component of agency and organizational plans working together. In practice, performance management often means *actively* using data to improve performance, including the strategic use of performance standards, measures, progress reports and ongoing quality improvement efforts to ensure an agency achieves desired results.[3] The PM System should consist of performance measures and indicators that represent how the health department is doing, the outcomes visible as part of agency efforts and the impacts being made. The PM System "tells a story" so to speak, the story of the health department or even a particular program. Think of a PM System from this perspective, the governor of the state or the local board of health calls the administrator of the health department and asks for a report or documentation that shows what the agency is doing with the $10.8 million that it is receiving each year for tobacco prevention. They also expect the report to demonstrate agency impacts in the community, and improvements in population health outcomes (the purpose behind receiving some of those funds). A health department who has a fully functioning PM System will be able to fulfill this request immediately. The PM System does not need to include everything that can be measured. It should, however, include anything meaningful to program impact and population health outcomes that can be measured. If the health department is doing something meaningful that is currently not being measured, it may take some creativity to measure, but *there is a way* for it to be measured and included in the PM System.

Beginning with the End in Mind

The PM System should include measures that represent the performance of the entire agency, agency plans and public health programs. A PM system *monitors performance*. The goal is to monitor programmatic and agency performance as often as possible. If progress is only reported on an annual basis, or in some cases, every 3–5 years, decisions cannot be made based on the information until after it has been reported. It is merely impossible to make substantial change within an agency, or improve performance, if the data is only being monitored annually. The PM System provides a centralized location to track important initiatives, allows for centralized reporting, and when updated and used correctly, allows for appropriate and timely decision making. Accurate performance measurement will generate data that demonstrates current performance, trend data and projected results. The key to timely decision making is in the frequency of reporting on performance measures and indicators. For measures that are updated monthly, if the results are not what the agency had hoped for or anticipated, it provides the ability to make timely operational changes based on current data. The system would then be monitored to watch for changes in the results (hopefully, for the better) in the following months. If a measure is updated annually, there is a longer waiting period to see results and if the information is used to guide decision-making about operational activities, it would then be another year to see if alterations had a positive outcome.

Conclusion

Lichiello and Turnock, the authors of *Guidebook for Performance Measurement* (1999) states that "Performance management is what you do with the information you've developed from measuring performance."[6] Designing a PM System gives agencies a structure and process for doing just that. This introductory chapter provides the rationale and foundations for PM System development and implementation. Actionable first steps were outlined for assessing the current situation, conducting a formal self-assessment and beginning plans for agency staff training to support the work. The resources provided throughout this book aim to strengthen capacity to lead this work.

References and Resources

1 Public Health Foundation. *Performance Management.* (n.d.). Retrieved December 3, 2019, from www.phf.org/focusareas/performancemanagement/Pages/Performance_Management.aspx

2 Public Health Foundation. *From Silos to Systems: Using Performance Management to Improve the Public's Health.* Retrieved November 25, 2019, from www.phf.org/resourcestools/Documents/silossystems.pdf

3 Public Health Foundation. (2013). *Performance Management Self-Assessment.* Retrieved from www.phf.org/focusareas/performancemanagement/toolkit/Pages/PM_Toolkit_Self_Assessment.aspx

4 Public Health Foundation. *Performance Management.* Retrieved May 30, 2018, from www.phf.org/focusareas/performancemanagement/Pages/Performance_Management.aspx?Topic=Performance+Management

5 Public Health Accreditation Board. (2013, December). *PHAB Standards and Measures, Version 1.5.* Retrieved December 2019, from www.phaboard.org: www.phaboard.org/wp-content/uploads/SM-Version-1.5-Board-adopted-FINAL-01-24-2014.docx.pdf

6 Lichiello, P. and Turnock, B. J. (1999). Guidebook for performance measurement. Seattle, WA: Turning Point.

7 Tower, C., Nostrand, E. V., Misra, R. and Barnett, D. J. (2019). Building Collective Efficacy to Support Public Health Workforce Development. *Journal of Public Health Management and Practice*, 1. doi: 10.1097/phh.0000000000000987

8 Rider, N., Frazier, C. M., Mckasson, S., Corso, L. and Mckeever, J. (2018). Achieving Public Health Standards and Increasing Accreditation Readiness. *Journal of Public Health Management and Practice*, 24(4), 392–399. doi: 10.1097/phh.0000000000000660

2 What is a Performance Management System?

What gets measured, gets managed.

(Peter Drucker)

Management, academics and practitioners often quote management guru Peter Drucker. The simple five-word phrase quoted above is short, makes intuitive sense and is alliterative. The wringing of hands regarding this adage includes:

1 Competing wisdom often attributed to Einstein: "Not everything that can be counted counts. Not everything that counts can be counted."[1]
2 Measurement alone does not result in management. Many have experienced the process of reporting data daily, weekly, monthly or quarterly only to see nothing done with those data.

Then, within the public health arena, many public health policy, systems and environment efforts truly are difficult to measure. And yet, measures are the foundation for performance management (PM). One challenge we face is that often, measures development begins and ends at the program level, perhaps as a result of funder reporting demands. These measures may align with agency strategic goals, but how can staff visualize and understand the connection between their work and the measures of their program with the larger mission of the organization. In the absence of a Performance Management System (PM System), one just has data. Data are relatively useless without context. Consequently, organizations need a process for collecting, sense-making and taking action on that data. "Performance management is what you do with the information you've developed from measuring performance."[2] Too often, "*what you do with the information*" is the part that gets lost. So, the PM System is a process and a system for taking action. Designing and developing a PM System is moving beyond the simplicity of measuring and moving toward systemic, informed decision-making. This chapter aims to explore three main questions:

1 What is a PM System?
2 How is the PM System developed and used?
3 Who contributes to the process?

What is a Performance Management System?

In 2015, the CDC's Center for State, Tribal, Local and Territorial Support (CSTLTS) created a history of activities that have fostered "awareness and use of performance management and quality improvement in public health."[3] This site provides a full look back at the history of PM development in public health, and it provides relevant resources for growing and developing the resources and networks for a PM professional. The CDC notes that the Turning Point Performance Management Collaborative was on the short list of key catalysts for developing the understanding of Performance Management that we have today. Further, this Turning Point work was the foundation for the Public Health Accreditation Board's requirement that state, local and tribal health departments develop PM Systems.

A fully functioning PM System that is completely integrated into health department daily practice at all levels includes: (1) setting organizational objectives across all levels of the department, (2) identifying indicators to measure progress toward achieving objectives on a regular basis, (3) identifying responsibility for monitoring progress and reporting, (4) identifying areas where achieving objectives requires focused quality improvement (QI) processes, and (5) visible leadership for ongoing PM. Department information systems and public health data support performance management.[4]

The Public Health Foundation released the refreshed Public Health Performance Management System Framework in 2013. This framework is referenced throughout this book.

The center of the PM System, is defining the four core elements:

- Performance Standards: Organizational or system expectations to improve public health practices based on internal or external goals or benchmarks.
- Performance Measures: Clearly defined indicators for collecting data to assess achievement of standards.
- Reporting of Progress: Documenting and analyzing results vs. expectations and communicating such information as feedback to guide future performance improvement decisions.
- Quality Improvement: A process to manage change and improve performance in public health policies, programs or infrastructure based on standards, data and reports.

The updates to those four core areas were described in an article: "Turning Point Revisited: Launching the Next Generation of Performance Management in Public Health."

Figure 2.1 Public Health Performance Management Framework.

In the revised framework, the four main components are displayed in a circle … to reflect the inherent cyclical nature of the process, consistent with continuous improvement. Double-headed arrows were incorporated into the circumference to emphasize that there could be multiple starting points for PM (i.e., an organization need not wait until all the components are in place to begin managing its performance). The Public Health Foundation added the fifth component, Visible Leadership.[5]

In that outer circle Public Health Performance Management System Framework, you can see additional concept that require planning and attention. For a PM System to be successful, agencies must also create conditions for "(1) cultivating a culture of quality, (2) aligning PM practices with the organization's strategic goals, (3) weighing customer experiences in program decisions or system changes, and (4) fostering transparency about organizational performance."[5]

How does the PM System Work Begin?

The Agency PM Cycle usually begins with a recognition of the importance of PM and the need for a PM System by the leadership. While these steps are the beginning, they are not the whole journey, but these steps cannot be skipped.

Typical Steps in Developing an Agency Performance Management Cycle

1. PM Training: Most public health practitioners received little to no training on how to design and align measures or how to think about the way the daily work fits into the system of the agency. Most agencies begin with training a core team to lead and champion this work; frequently using consultants, as ASTHO mentions in their Performance Management Leadership Guide.[6] The training of staff is absolutely critical. The authors have worked with many public health agencies, and as a result have observed many processes. Learning the PM System design and implementation is difficult and requires training support. The training process can also support team development and cohesion.
2. Select Goals Aligned with Strategic Plan: As mentioned in Chapter 1, the PM System should be a system that tracks progress on the strategic goals of the agency, which means there should be alignment in the PM System with the agency strategic plan.
3. Develop/Review SMART Objectives: Most programs are already measuring dozens of indicators of success. This process focuses the work through prioritizing and revisiting best practices measures design: Specific, Measurable, Attainable, Realistic and Time-bound. A key component here is discovering the program objectives that align with the division or department's strategic goals.
4. Develop/Review Strategies and Activities based on Evidence: This is a return to looking at the Performance Standards. All too often, seemingly good ideas get generated to design creative interventions, and this step reminds program managers of the need for evidence based interventions.
5. Develop/Review Measures and Targets: We'll revisit this in a later chapter, but a key to PM System design is knowing what the target is. Data need context to clarify when progress is being made.
6. Collect Data: This is part of the process design. Once key indicators have been selected, who will do this data collection?
7. Report Data: And once data are collected, where will those data be submitted/housed?

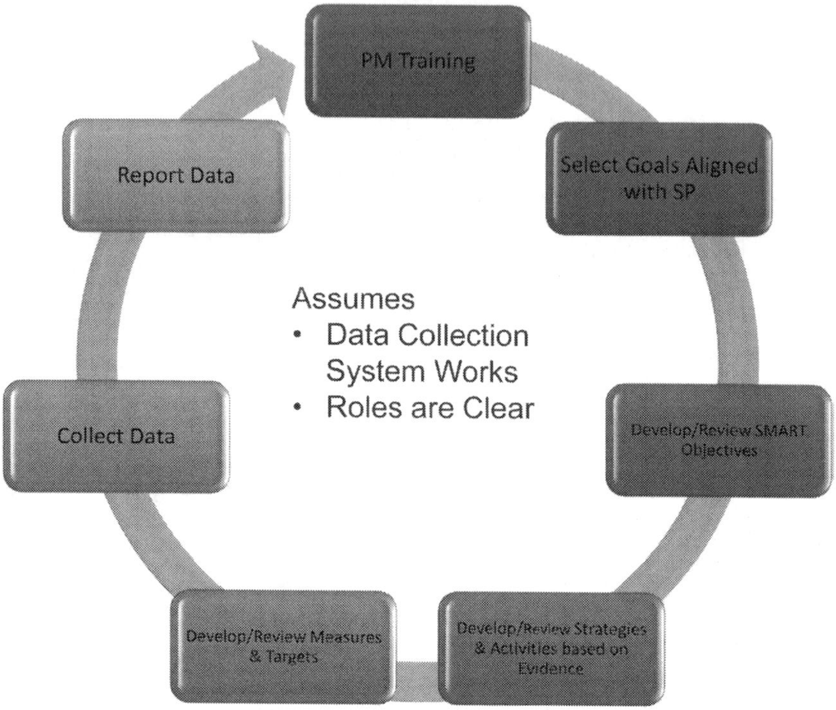

Figure 2.2 Typical Agency Performance Management Cycle.

These seven steps require so much time and energy to build those PM System foundations that often the critical success of *using the data* gets lost, at least in the beginning stages.

How can a PM System be Used in an Organization?

There are several steps to PM System action once the data have been selected, collected and reported. Challenges happen when agencies fail to plan for how they will regularly: convene the team, analyze the data, make decisions, recommend actions and determine how QI fits into their process. Agencies that have designed and developed the first seven steps above really hit their PM System strides when they have a process for convening and using the data.

Full Agency PM Action Cycle

Convene PM Team: Organizations need a Performance Management Team. For those seeking PHAB accreditation, this is a requirement. This does not have to be a new committee, though based on agency size, it might be. In some agencies this is the leadership team or the Quality Improvement Team, or a combination of these groups. Often the PM Team/Council includes the program leaders who are contributing the data. This will be discussed further in Chapter 6.

- Analyze Data: When agencies begin this work, the process of just reporting is such a herculean effort that often, all energy is directed simply to the data collection efforts. If the system has been designed to collect key measures and compare them against targets, then additional analysis can be made through the convening and discussion process. Chapter 5 includes a list of questions that the PM Team/Council might consider for their discussion, review and analysis.
- Make Informed Decisions and Recommend Actions: Perhaps the best advantage from this PM System work comes from the opportunity to analyze, understand and make new data-informed choices. Based on the data available through the PM System, and through the analysis process,

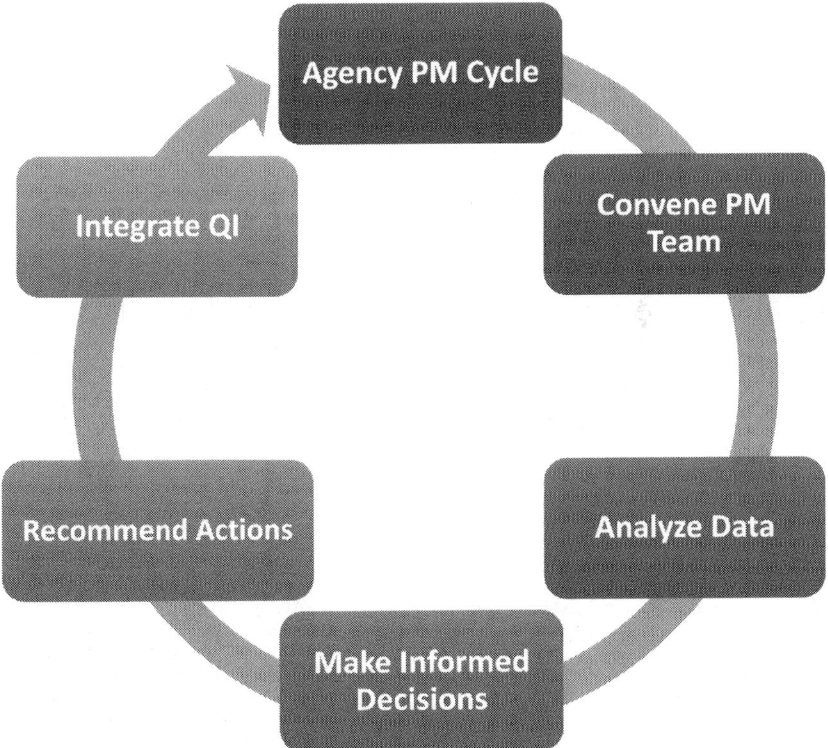

Figure 2.3 The Full Performance Management Process.

agencies can consider new initiatives, discover needs for changes in staffing models, strategically seek new funds based on demand and even discover work that may be best accomplished through partner agencies.

- Integrate QI: The data generated through strategic PM System efforts provides the foundation for selecting QI initiatives. A team that is meeting and studying the data can use data for decisions to improve policies, programs and outcomes; manage changes; and create a learning organization.

Who Should be Involved in the Agency's PM System Process?

This chapter has looked at *what* the PM System is and *how* the PM System gets started. This section focuses on who should be involved. In short, involve as many people as possible as often as possible. People like to understand the purpose of what they are doing. When people are involved in selecting measures, delivering on those goals and measuring they process, "buy-in" is naturally created. PHAB Standards provide a best practice set of standards to follow. PHAB prepared for an updated version of the *Standards and Measures 2.0 by* creating a "lessons learned" report from agencies who struggled to meet the staff engagement measures. The report included:

Performance on Measure 9.1.1 (in both Versions 1.0 and 1.5) requires that staff be engaged in establishing and/or updating a PM System. The most common challenges are (1) insufficient documentation of leadership engagement, (2) insufficient documentation of staff engagement, and (3) staff not engaged in the development or updating of the PM System.[6]

Once agency leadership have agreed on the organizing principles of goals and objectives, program teams can generate their most reliable and responsive measures that can be included in the PM System. Staff from programs across the agency can be responsible for updating their key indicators. There are many ways to creatively share PM System results on a recurring basis.

Conclusion

A public health Performance Management System does not refer to the employee performance review process. As ASTHO's Performance Management Leadership Guide notes, "The PM System, in advanced stages, regularly drives decision making, influences the allocation of resources, and highlights the department's priorities."[7] A PM System is not simply collecting data, and often that part of the work is not so simple. It is not an elaborate effort to rearrange current data collection methods to create a pretty spreadsheet or dashboard. PM involves both a process and an output. Confidently answering "yes" to the following prompts is a good beginning and a clear step toward assessing whether the agency has a PM System:

1 There are defined processes and methods for choosing performance *standards*, indicators or targets.
2 Managers and employees are held accountable for meeting standards and targets.
3 Data are collected on the measures on an established schedule.
4 There are defined methods and criteria for selecting performance *measures*.
5 Reports on progress are clear, relevant and current so people can understand and use them for decision-making (e.g., PM dashboard).
6 Leaders are effective in communicating performance outcomes to the public to demonstrate effective use of public dollars.
7 There is a process or mechanism to coordinate QI efforts among groups that share the same performance targets.
8 Performance data are used to select and implement QI projects.
9 There is a team responsible for integrating PM effort.

References and Resources

1 O'Toole, G. (2010, May 26). *Not Everything That Counts Can Be Counted.* Retrieved from Quote Investigator: https://quoteinvestigator.com/2010/05/26/everything-counts-einstein/
2 Lichiello, P. (n.d.). *Guidebook for Performance Measurement.* Retrieved from Public Health Foundation: www.phf.org/resourcestools/Documents/PMCguidebook.pdf
3 CDC. (2015, November 9). *Performance Management and Quality Improvement.* Retrieved June 2018, from cdc.gov: www.cdc.gov/stltpublichealth/performance/journey.html
4 Public Health Accreditation Board. (2013, December). *PHAB Standards and Measures, Version 1.5.* Retrieved 2018, from www.phaboard.org: www.phaboard.org/wp-content/uploads/SM-Version-1.5-Board-adopted-FINAL-01-24-2014.docx.pdf
5 DeAngelo, J. W., Beitsch, L. M., Beaudry, M. L., Corzo, L. C., Estes, L. J. and Bialek, R. G. (2014, Sep–Oct). *J Public Health Manag Pract.* 2014 Sep–Oct; 20(5): 463–471. Turning Point Revisited: Launching the Next Generation of Performance Management in Public Health Julia W. DeAngelo, MPH, Leslie M. Beitsch, MD, JD, Margaret L. Beaudry, MA, Liza C. Corso, MPA,). Turning Point Revisited: Launching the Next Generation of Performance Management in Public Health. *J Public Health Manag Pract.*, 20(5), 463–471.
6 Public Health Accreditation Board. (2018, August). *VERSION 2.0 WORK IN PROGRESS: Quality Improvement/Performance Management – What Have We Learned from Accredited Health Departments.* Retrieved from phaboard.org: www.phaboard.org/wp-content/uploads/2.0QIPMLearned.pdf
7 Association of State and Territorial Health Officials. (2017, April). *Performance Management Leadership Guide.* Retrieved 2019, from Association of State and Territorial Health Officials: www.astho.org/Accreditation-and-Performance/Performance-Management-Leadership-Guide/Home/

3 Introducing Performance Management to an Organization

Performance Management (PM) is change management. For many agencies, introducing a system-wide system is change, sharing program performance measures outside the programs themselves is a change, and discussing how to improve – with partners outside the programs – is a change. This process needs to be managed carefully from the outset. The way the concept of PM is introduced will impact how successful it is.

Whenever a major organizational transformation is made, failure is always a concern. Failure can be costly, especially when these transformations are large in scope. Failure can be monetary (loss of investment costs), affect professional development (poor performance review), affect morale (stress of not executing effectively), create waste (staff time, new equipment purchased and not used) or impact the entire system (software catastrophe). If the focus of change is on launching the transformation, an important question can be missed: "How do we ensure this works?"

Change Management Contingency Matrix

To make sure a major organization transformation works the first time it is suggested, a Change Management Contingency Matrix can be used. It is especially useful when an organization, division or program is contemplating a major change in the way things are being done. The Change Management Contingency Matrix is used in order to preemptively evaluate potential areas for failure and designing a plan for avoiding them. The Change Management Contingency Matrix is shown in Figure 3.1.

To develop a Change Management Contingency Matrix, start by brainstorming a list of the key characteristics that will create success in the potential transformation such as:

- Management support at all levels
- Clear and timely communication to all levels about the transformation

Transformation Contingency Success Matrix

Potential Failure Examples	High	Medium	Low	N/A	How To Overcome	Status
1.						✔ – Ready
2.						X – Not ready
3.						☼ – Good Progress
4.						
5.						
6.						
7.						
8.						
9.						
10.						
11.						

Figure 3.1 Transformation Contingency Success Matrix Template.

- Employee buy-in
- Adequate time to develop necessary employee skills

Next, determine and describe the opposite of each characteristic identified. List these in the first column of the Change Management Contingency Matrix as follows:

- Lack of management support at all levels
- Poor communications
- Lack of employee engagement and understanding
- No time to develop skill sets

Rate each of the potential failures on its probability of occurrence, from high to low. Place an X in the box that best corresponds to probability for each of the potential failures. Use the N/A (not applicable) column if any of the potential failures are determined not to apply to this transformation.

Then for each potential failure, identify a strategy to overcome or prevent it. Add these strategies to the Change Management Contingency Matrix, as seen in the example in Figure 3.2.

On a regular basis, monitor progress on implementing the strategies for preventing or overcoming the potential failures. Once the status of all of the

Transformation Contingency Success Matrix

Potential Failure Examples	High	Medium	Low	N/A	How To Overcome	Status
1. No Senior Management Involvement	X				Build sense of urgency and conviction	✔ – Ready
2. No Defined Phasing of the Transformation		X			Clear Define each Phase and its Objectives	X – Not ready
3. No Clear Owner for Each Phase		X			Develop a guiding coalition	☼ – Good Progress
4. Lack of Rollout Process	X				Develop the practical steps to follow	
5. No Time for Training		X			Find Creative Ways to Build Needed Skills	
6. Lack of a Communication Plan	X				Develop the Transformation Vision And New Culture	
7. No Stakeholder Involvement		X			Start Focus Groups	
8. Clear Value to Stakeholders to Participate	X				Develop Value Proposition	
9. A Clear Quality/ Efficiency Improvement	X				Define What We Gain From the Transformation	
10. No Defined Change Agents		X			Build and Train a Pool at All Levels	
11. Others					Specifics to Your Organization	

Figure 3.2 Transformation Contingency Success Matrix Example.

potential failures has changed to “Ready” or “Good Progress Being Made,” implement the transformation.

Experience shows that the majority of employees go through the eight stages of “resistance to acceptance” cycle. See Stages of Resistance table.

Some members of the organization never get past the first stage, some experience most of these stages of resistance. Most make it to the acceptance stage and become comfortable with the new way.

Table 3.1 8 Stages of Resistance

Stage	*Response*
Shock	Overwhelmed. This seems impossible.
Denial	There is no need for this.
Anger	Why are they pushing this?
Confusion	What is this change supposed to accomplish?
Depression	This will disrupt daily work and routines.
Crisis	I may have to find a new job since I do not have the new skills needed. I will not make it in the new environment.
Exploration	Training has provided the skills to try the new way.
Acceptance	The process is working well.

Change Management

As the change leader, the goal is to move the organization's personnel as quickly as possible through the eight stages by providing the necessary clear communications about what PM is, when the system will be operational, how the PM System will be used initially, what training and support will be available to develop the necessary skills to use it, and meetings that will be held to answer questions. Employees' willingness to change is a combination of cognitive (understanding the reason for the change) and emotional (reaction based on past experience) buy-in to the change. The communication messages must appeal to both since they interact with each other and are needed to get people to move through the eight stages of the resistance to acceptance cycle.

Managing Culture Change

Changing an organization's entrenched culture is not a simple task, especially when measurement is involved. The change leader needs to understand that this is a difficult task. While it takes an investment of time and energy, systemic management of performance has a huge potential payoff. The change leader must build the belief in the organization for the need for change. This is done by delivering a clear and consistent message on why the change is needed and what it entails. This consistent message helps continually build the belief at all levels in the organization for the need to change. This increasing belief helps spread the adoption and ownership of the change. Shared ownership of the of the PM System relies on ownership and when both are in place, this influences culture. When the change leader manages a trustworthy process with intention and transparency, the result can include new social capital within the agency among both leadership and agency staff.

The change leader must work diligently to unlock the fixed mindset in the organization against any change to one that is a growth mindset open to new approaches and a willingness to change. This takes persistence on the change leader's part to get the organization unstuck and open to new ways of doing business which is what PM is all about.

Managing the Personalities

The Change Management Personality Matrix, shown in Figure 3.3, is a tool to help determine, before making a change, what kinds of resistance and support to the change may be encountered. When starting a change initiative, it is useful to gauge what could potentially be the employee's response to a proposed change initiative. It is helpful to see how these personality archetypes may influence the process by considering the *Change Management Personality Matrix.*

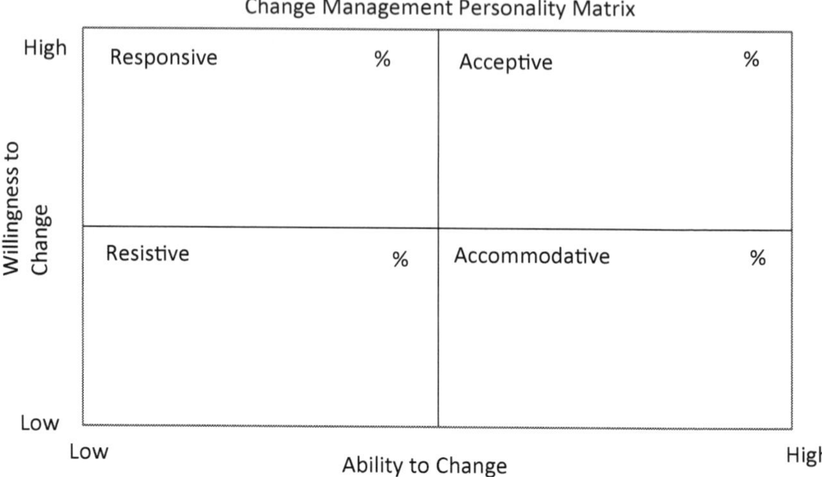

Figure 3.3 Change Management Personality Matrix Template.

The types of personalities described in the Change Management Personality Matrix are as follows:

Resistive Types – These types tend to fear any change since it upsets the status quo that they are comfortable with. They will usually argue that the change is unclear, they were not consulted (if they were consulted they probably would not participate). The main reason is they feel threatened and feel they are losing more than they would gain with the change being proposed. The only way the resistive type starts to somewhat support the change is when they feel there is no other option – other than leaving the organization.

Responsive Types – These types tend to deal in real time and not the future. They tend to respond to what they see the majority of the organization is doing. If the majority of the organization is rejecting change they will jump on board. However, if they can be convinced that the change is good, they have a high willingness to support it. On their own, they usually do not have the ability to change but with training and coaching this can be overcome.

Accommodative Types – These types tend to have the ability to change but not the willingness. They usually feel overwhelmed by the current workload and do not have any energy left to take on anything else. To get them to be more willing they need to see the personal benefits the change will bring to them from actively engaging in the change.

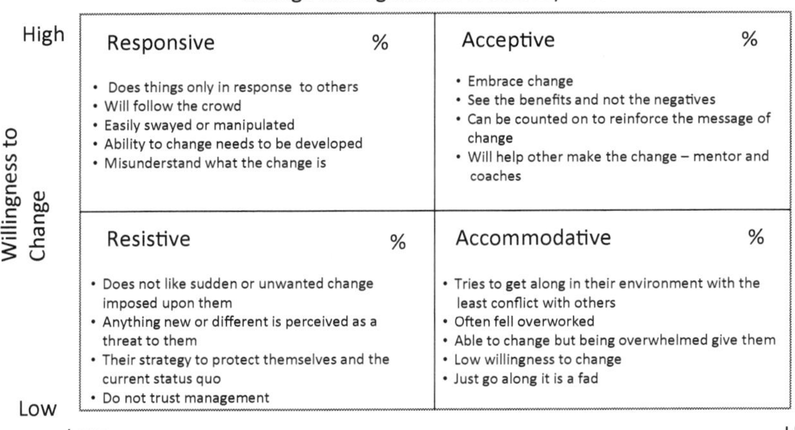

Figure 3.4 Change Management Personality Matrix Example.

> *Progressive Types* – These types tend to embrace change since they usually see the benefits outweigh any negatives the change may cause. They are usually the forward thinkers in the organization and can be counted on to help reinforce the reason why we have to change. They usually are supportive of the Responsive and Accommodative Types to help them make the change.

Naming the challenges-together as a team- is a useful tool for managing change. This matrix helps the entire change team understand what they are up against. It may be a useful exercise to estimate what percent of the organization is in each of the four quadrants based on past change efforts. These results can inform the types of communication messaging needed to address each type of personality.

Communication Planning for Introducing PM System

When PM is being introduced to the organization, make sure that the initial communications do the following as a minimum:

- Clearly define the reasons and the need for the change to minimize the fear of the unknown people may have. This will build up trust in the organization that this change is well planned out and will be easily executed.
- Explain how people will get the needed skills and support to function in the new environment.

- Indicate when overview sessions will be held and when people can comment on the approach – make them feel part of the process.
- Define the benefits of making the change to the individual and the organization.

After the initial introductions to the plans for a new PM System have been launched, a survey could be done to see what the attitude is to the proposed change across the organization. Once that is complete the matrix can be updated with the results and another round of messaging can be developed to continue to reduce resistance. Communication is a key to the trustworthy process and must be a continuous part of the implementation strategy.

Conclusion

Managing a change process requires noticing the people in the process and the natural process of resistance to change. Knowing how the resistance is segmented will help to determine what type of communications are needed to address each type of personality.

Remember, employees' willingness to change is a combination of cognitive (understanding the reason for the change) and emotional (reaction based on past experience) buy-in to the change. The communication messages must appeal to both since they interact with each other and are needed to get people to move through the eight stages of the resistance to acceptance cycle.

Designing, installing and deploying a PM System takes a great deal of planning to ensure it has high initial acceptance early on by the majority of the employees in the organization. A PM System is of great value to any organization by providing periodic, repeatable cycles of information the organization can use to continually improve its operating performance. A good PM System is the central nervous system of the organization since it is providing operational intelligence on a real time basis, indicating performance relative to goals, effectiveness and efficiency of programs and services, performance of processes, and customer satisfaction levels. Over time, the PM System should provide the knowledge leadership requires to manage the overall organization and to aid in prioritizing which areas need improvements.

Bibliography

Moran, J. W. and McCarty, A. (2018, January). Change Management Contingency Matrix. Retrieved November 13, 2019, from www.phf.org/resourcestools/Pages/Change_Management_Contingency_Matrix.asp

Moran, J. W. (2018, May 25). Four Secrets for Leading Successful Change. Retrieved November 13, 2019, from www.processexcellencenetwork.com/people-performance-and-change-in-process-improveme/articles/four-secrets-of-change-management/

Moran, J. W. and Beitsch, L. (2016, November 1). Are You Really Ready to Make A Change? Retrieved from www.processexcellencenetwork.com/organizational-change/articles/are-you-really-ready-to-make-a-change

Moran, J. W. and Beitsch, L. (2017, April). Change Management Questionnaire Checklist. Retrieved from www.phf.org/resourcestools/Pages/Change_Management_Questionnaire_Checklist.aspx

Armbruster, S., Moran, J. and Beitsch, L. (2013) "Change Resistors: People Who Block Change Initiatives and 5 Tips to Overcome Resistance." *Journal of Public Health Management and Practice* 19(5), 483–484.

4 The Five Stages of Performance Management

Organizations have long struggled with developing a Performance Management System to help understand, chapter, track and improve the organization's operations. While many organizations use some form of performance measurement, far fewer have successfully completed the transition to a PM System which integrates performance measurement from the Health Improvement Plan, Strategic Plan and the Operational Plans into the ongoing management of the organization. This transition is much more difficult than the initial development of performance measures.[1]

The Public Health Performance Management Framework[2] discussed in Chapter 2 was developed specifically for public health. This chapter supplements the Public Health Performance Management Framework by providing guidance about stages of Performance Management (PM) practice. Specifically, this chapter addresses:

- Selecting standards
- Measuring and determining the status of standards
- Reporting measurement data
- Prioritizing areas needing improvement
- Developing a system that helps improve the efficiency and effectiveness of the organization

Consulting with state, tribal, local and territorial health departments has provided the authors with insight into how PM develops over time. This has led to articulating five progressive stages of PM practice. Each stage will be described, including general characteristics, guidance on how to transition to the next stage and resources available to help in the transition. In addition to elements outlined in the Public Health Performance Management Framework, components of a fully integrated culture of PM System include:

- Continuous staff training
- A clear standardized process to gather and analyze the data

- A process for revising measures
- Using the PM system as a tool to strengthen alignment of agency plans (health assessment, health improvement plans, Quality Improvement (QI) plans, workforce development plans and strategic plan)
- Continually build trust in the agency on how the measurement will be used to drive continuous improvement
- Adequate staffing
- Action based on results
- Constant communication

Seeing the full progression helps a health department understand where it is starting from and the strategies needed to transition to the next stage, as shown in Figure 4.1.

Approaching the responsibility of leading and implementing agency PM can feel like learning to drive. Suddenly a simple idea – driving a car – demands a constant interplay of decisions, skills, rules and coordination. Thankfully, driver training breaks this daunting challenge into more manageable tasks, starting with mirror and seat adjustments and calling attention to components one might not have considered before. Similarly, PM has subtle complexities that are hard to notice at the outset. An agency that has visible leadership and training systems in place may not have the process for managing and collecting the data; conversely, the best data collection system still breaks down if there is no leadership to do something with the information. This chapter does not provide agencies with a PM score; rather, it provides a

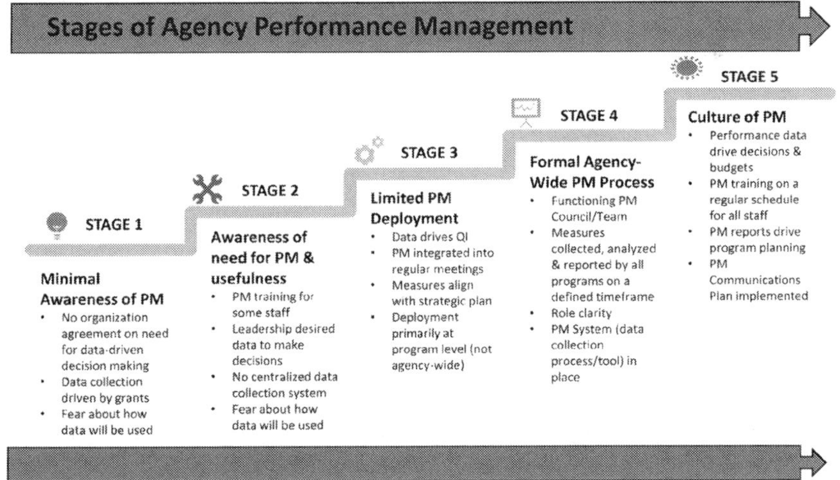

Figure 4.1 Stages of Agency Performance Management.

framework for noticing and assessing agency characteristics, and then taking action to enable transition to the next stage of PM practice.

The five stages of Agency Performance Management are described in detail below.

Stage 1: Minimal Awareness of PM

Characteristics of Stage 1

- Organization does not see the need for measurement data to make decisions
- Leadership does not request or rely on data to make decisions
- Crisis management is the operation mode
- Programs function in silos
- Data is collected primarily for grant reporting purposes
- Employees fear how management will use measurement data
- Lack of transparency

Transition Strategies to Stage 2

- Senior management education and training events
- Study examples of successful organizations use of PM Systems
- Build trust in the process through team building exercises and continuous communication
- Emphasize PHAB Standards

Resources for Stage 1

- Examples of other agency uses of PM[4,5,6]
- Public Health Performance Management System Framework[2,3]
- Getting Started with Performance Management[7]

Stage 2: Awareness of the Need for PM and Its Usefulness

Characteristics of Stage 2

- Leadership wants to get out of the crisis mode of operation and begin making data-driven decisions
- Staff in leadership positions have attended local, state or national conferences/trainings with a focus on PM
- PM has become a topic on intermittent leadership agendas
- Measures are primarily focused on grant requirements
- No centralized data collection system exists
- Employees still fear how measurement will be used

Transition Strategies to Stage 3

- Conduct an agency PM self-assessment[8] to raise team members' awareness about the complexity and elements of PM, pockets of comparatively advanced PM practice, as well as areas needing development
- Conduct a basic PM training for leadership and start to sell the idea
- Develop a vocabulary of the most common data management terms
- Conduct training for measures design – Goals/Targets/Outcomes
- Adopt a simple process for managing data (spreadsheets, electronic dashboard, etc.)

Resources for Stage 2

- Getting Started with Performance Management[7]
- Subscribe to newsletters like *Performance Improvement Inside Track*[9]
- Join to the Public Health Performance Improvement Network[10]

Stage 3: Limited PM Deployment

Characteristics of Stage 3

- Senior management and program level management use program data to drive selection of QI projects
- PM is a standing agenda item for all program level meetings
- Programs have defined measures to assess progress aligned with strategic plan
- There is clear accountability for measures collection
- At the program level, data are collected on a regular schedule
- Data are analyzed to look for opportunities for improvement
- Effort has been applied to draft a PM Plan

Transition Strategies to Stage 4

- Dedicate increased staff time (both a lead/coordinator and time at all programmatic levels) to develop measures and manage the data collection and analysis process
- Convene leadership team to review adoption of performance measurement and review among programs and identify gaps
- Conduct an inventory of measures being used across the agency; look for duplication; look for numbers of output, process and outcomes measures and their alignment
- Appoint and empower a data management coordinator
- Begin aligning program measures with agency strategic goals

Resources for Stage 3

- Performance Management and Cultural Transformation Using PDCA[11]

Stage 4: Formal Agency-Wide PM Process

Characteristics of Stage 4

- A PM Plan has been written, approved by senior management and implemented
- A formal council or leadership team meets to review the measures and how the PM System is functioning.
- Leadership regularly reports on the PM process through agency communications or all-staff meetings.
- PM is a standing agenda item for all senior leadership level meetings
- Measures have defined targets based in evidence or standards
- Measures are aligned with the agency's strategic plan
- Measures are collected on a defined timeframe (monthly/quarterly etc.)
- Staff roles are clear regarding data collection and reporting
- There is a system – data collection tool – in place (Excel spreadsheet on a shared drive, electronic dashboard) and these data drive QI project selection

Transition to Stage 5 Strategies

- Use the results from the agency PM self-assessment to build action plans
- Create and implement a PM communications plan
- Adequate staff time is dedicated to data management

Resource for Stage 4

- Competencies for Performance Improvement Professionals in Public Health[12]

Stage 5: Culture of PM

Characteristics of Stage 5

- Performance data are used to make strategic decisions related to staffing, budgets or new initiatives
- Staff present the process or outcomes of agency performance improvement efforts at state, regional or national conferences
- Measures are visible throughout the agency

- Measure review and refinement occur regularly
- PM training occurs on a regular basis for all relevant staff positions
- Reports pulled from the system are a daily tool for programs
- The PM and QI process is detailed in a policy/procedure/plan

Resources for Stage 5

- PHF's Performance Management Toolkit[13]
- NACCHO's Chapter to Communicating about Performance Improvement[14]

Conclusion

Implementing a PM system is fundamentally about closely examining the system, and strategically re-designing it to match the organization's mission and goals. Such redesigns and transitions are hard. The first step is to be clear about your purpose and intention. This chapter offers incremental transition strategies to help an organization move through these progressive stages toward a culture of PM. Using this framework can help keep an organization's PM practice evergreen and responsive to dynamic variables.

There is no one PM System that fits all. Each organization needs to develop a system that fits their leadership and management needs, is easy to use, and reinforces a culture of PM and improvement.

References and Resources

1 *Performance Management and Cultural Transformation Using PDCA*: www.phf.org/news/Pages/Performance_Management_and_Cultural_Transformation_Using_PDCA.aspx
2 Public Health Performance Management Framework: www.phf.org/focusareas/performancemanagement/toolkit/Pages/PM_Toolkit_About_the_Performance_Management_Framework.aspx
3 Turning Point: Performance Management Project and Publications: www.phf.org/resourcestools/Pages/Turning_Point_Project_Publications.aspx
4 NACCHO Local Public Health PM Examples: www.naccho.org/programs/public-health-infrastructure/performance-improvement/performance-management
5 ASTHO State PM Case Studies: www.astho.org/Programs/Accreditation-and-Performance/Resources-and-Tools/
6 PHF Examples of Performance Management in Practice: www.phf.org/focusareas/performancemanagement/toolkit/Pages/PM_Toolkit_Examples_of_Performance_Management_in_Practice.aspx
7 Getting Started with Performance Management: www.phf.org/focusareas/performancemanagement/toolkit/Pages/PM_Toolkit_Getting_Started.aspx
8 Performance Management Self-Assessment: www.phf.org/focusareas/performancemanagement/toolkit/Pages/PM_Toolkit_Self_Assessment.aspx

9 *Performance Improvement Inside Track:* www.phf.org/insidetrack
10 Performance Improvement Network: www.phpinetwork.org/
11 *Performance Management and Cultural Transformation Using PDCA*: www.phf.org/news/Pages/Performance_Management_and_Cultural_Transformation_Using_PDCA.aspx
12 Competencies for Performance Improvement Professionals in Public Health: www.phf.org/programs/performanceimprovement/Pages/Performance_Improvement_Competencies_Public_Health.aspx
13 PHF Performance Management Toolkit: www.phf.org/focusareas/performancemanagement/toolkit/Pages/Performance_Management_Toolkit.aspx
14 NACCHO *Guide to Communicating About Performance Improvement*: http://archived.naccho.org/topics/infrastructure/accreditation/picommunications.cfm

5 Developing Agency and Programmatic Goals, Objectives, Measures and Targets

Stephen Covey, in his best-selling book, *Seven Habits of Highly Effective People*, stated that one of the seven habits of effective people is their commitment to "begin with the end in mind."[1] Often, people describe the output of the Performance Management System (PM System) as a dashboard. If that is the "end" or the output from the PM System efforts, perhaps that metaphor needs a closer look. Sticking with the previous example of learning to drive a car, the dashboard on cars has several standard dials and newer cars have dozens of indicator lights. These are all important to the subsystems that make up the car. However, for daily management of the car, drivers primarily watch the speed and the gas gauge. These are vital for just-in-time measurements. Other systems are still being monitored and need to be measured, like tire pressure and engine temperature; and there are times when those measures are critical and the data are needed for management. With this in mind, as performance managers are selecting objectives and measures to include in the agency dashboard, the challenge is working across the agency to find those measures that matter to decision-making and management at the *agency* level. This process of designing and selecting presses performance managers to appreciate that some measures may continue to be important for collecting and reporting to funders, however, those measures may not be the strategic measures selected for the agency PM System.

Another look at the standards for PM System development can ground the process. The Public Health Accreditation Board's Standards and Measures (v. 1.5) provide a standard for all local, state, tribal and territorial health departments, regardless of their intention to apply for accreditation. In Measure 9.1.2, the significance of the measure is described as:

> A performance management system encompasses all aspects of using objectives and measurement to evaluate the performance of programs, policies, and processes, and achievement of outcome targets. An adopted performance management system communicates across the department

> how the department will (1) ensure that goals are being met consistently in an effective and efficient manner and (2) identify the need to improve organizational results.[2]

This description offers expectations without specifics. Health departments are uniquely organized and provide a breadth of services appropriate to the needs of their populations. Thus, every public health PM System is unique. *Standards & Measures* offers clear guidance about what is meant by a PM System, but this document says nothing about how to achieve this outcome. This chapter aims to provide guidance about how to begin the process.

This development work is challenging for many reasons. First, this work relies on critical thinking about what will actually matter and make a difference. This requires a review of current practices and consideration about how those stack up against best practices. Second, this work absolutely requires teamwork. While nearly all employees want to think of themselves as team players, it is well documented that working in teams gets the best results, it also takes longer. Working effectively with a team is the subject of many other books, so while this is not addressed here, recognizing the role and importance of teamwork cannot be overlooked. This work requires critical choices about what will be tracked. Third, all staff want their work to matter, and therefore all staff need to see their work, or understand how their work is reflected in the PM System. Finally, this work takes time and training to equip staff to be ready for the effort, and time and training are precious resources. Therefore, given the challenges, one's purpose for engaging in this work must be clear. In the development process, agency staff must come together to define the benefits and create their own reasons for "buy-in."

Overview of Goals and Objectives

A goal is an abstract and general umbrella statement, under which specific objectives can be clustered. A goal is an overarching principle that guides decision making. Most agencies develop three to five goals as part of their strategic planning process. In fact, the *PHAB Standards & Measures* document requires that this work be completed as part of the strategic planning process in Measure 5.3.2 which states: "The health department's goals and objectives with measurable and time-framed targets (expected products or results). Measurable and time-framed targets may be contained in another document…."[2] The PM System can provide the mechanism for tracking these goals developed in the strategic planning process. Another key consideration related to goals selection is the thoughtful consideration of control. A PM System needs to be related to the performance of the agency. While the mission of the agency is related to improving the health of the community, the Health Assessment (CHA/SHA/THA) and Health Improvement Plan

(CHIP/SHIP/THIP) are the plans for documenting and managing those aims and outcomes. The broad strategic goals for the agency need to focus on the performance of the agency, the matters under the agency's control.

Objectives are statements that describe – in precise, measurable and attainable terms – defined and desired outcomes. Objectives are specific, measurable steps that can be taken to meet the goal. For each goal statement, an agency may want to monitor three to five objectives that, if met, will result in a high likelihood of positively influencing the goal. For example, if the goal is to reduce chronic disease in the community, will counting the number of tobacco quitline brochures really be the best measure? When paired with the measures, objectives should make clear who will do what by when and by how much.

Overview of Measures

Performance measures are the specific quantitative representations of the capacity, process or outcome that is being assessed. As Figure 5.1 illustrates, performance measures must be discrete (defined only for an isolated set of points). They must also be measurable, which sounds obvious, but public health is often trying to impact concepts that are difficult to measure like equity, health behaviors, engagement or empowerment. Thus, time must be spent and care must be taken to discover and design meaningful measures. Working around the concentric circles, performance measures of agency effectiveness are often closer to the center. The intention is to select measures

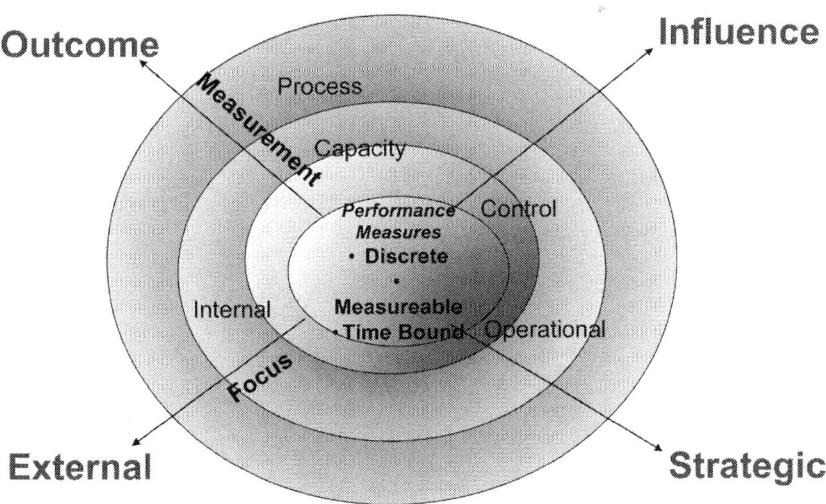

Figure 5.1 Performance Measures Continuum.

that can be controlled, regarding operations, focused on internal efforts, and related to capacity and process. This work must be done with a continuous focus on how effectiveness with those measures will positively influence health, lead to strategic goals, assure the agency is effective with external partners and reach the outcomes defined in the health improvement plans. Use evidence to show that improving results on output or process measures really does drive outcomes, or develop new measures and targets that have an evidence-base, or use the PDCA cycle to develop the evidence base. We have included a worksheet template as Figure A.2 in the Appendix to help guide initial discussions on developing draft goals, objectives and supporting performance measures. The template is meant to help keep the team focused on developing priority goals, supporting objectives and related performance measures. A completed environmental health program example of the template is also provided in Figure A.3 in the Appendix.

One way to approach measures design is to think about levels:

- How much are we doing? (capacity/output)
    - Output measures include numbers of services provided, the number of customers served and the level of activity to provide services.
- How effectively are we doing? How well did we do? (process)
    - Process measures report timeliness, cost effectiveness or quality measures.
- Who cares? Is anyone better off? (outcomes)
    - Outcome measures assess program impact and effectiveness and show whether expected results are achieved.

These questions can help teams connect their current work and measures to a performance measures development mindset.

According to the *Guidebook for Performance Measurement*,[3] key attributes of performance measures include:

> **Validity** … a valid measure is one that captures the essence of what it professes to measure.
>
> **Reliability** … a reliable measure has a high likelihood of yielding the same results in repeated trials, so there are low levels of random error in measurement.
>
> **Responsiveness** … a responsive measure should be able to detect change.

Functionality … a functional measure is directly related to objectives.

Credibility … a credible measure is supported by stakeholders.

Understandability … an understandable measure is easily understood by all, with minimal explanation.

Availability … an available measure is readily available through the means on hand.

Abuse-Proof … an abuse-proof measure is unlikely to be used against that which is, or those who are, measured.[3]

The following questions, developed by the National State Auditors Association, can serve as another tool to help develop performance measures, and then revise each performance measure:

1 Is it meaningful?
2 Is it focused on customer needs and demands?
3 Is it accurate and are reliable data available?
4 Is it simple enough to be understood?
5 Is it cost effective to collect and report the data?
6 Can the data be compared over time?
7 Is the measure compatible with other performance measures?
8 Is the measure useful to others?

Overview of Targets

A set of performance measures should compare actual performance with expected results. The work of setting targets is often a stumbling block for teams new to performance measures. The setting of the target can be an opportunity for increased clarity about the measures development process. A simple personal example comes from a desire to move more and eat better. Public health professionals promote healthy lifestyles all the time, and it is the specificity and setting of targets that begins to make a difference for individuals. For example, what does it mean to move more? More than what? This could be measured by many in steps counters or minutes of participation in moderate or high impact cardiovascular programs. At a simple level, many have seen a goal of 10,000 steps per day. That's a target. And if a person is starting with a baseline of 3,000 steps per day, the target may need to be lower. These targets can be based on best practices or past performance. Sometimes it makes sense to set a target that is 10 percent higher than last year, but if staffing has not changed and the measure is not affected by efficiency, it is possible that a target may best remain at a previous year's measure. Further, an agency may be working with partners to shift a responsibility for a service, and therefore, a goal may be to decrease. The aim is to engage in meaningful dialogue with the team to find targets that make sense and if met, will impact the goal.

Figure 5.2 below is an example of a dashboard for one goal, one objective for that goal and three measures designed to impact the goal. For each, there is a target defined by the "period" which could be monthly or quarterly, depending on the agency. These are followed by trend lines to see visually how the actual progress data is measuring up to the planned targets.

Additional examples of performance management dashboards can be found in the Appendix, Figures A.4 and A.5.

Examples in Practice of Goal, Objective, Measure Alignment

Public Health Program Measures

The PM System reports on what the public health agency determines to be a top priority and included in the system. Just because programs, initiatives and activities are not listed in the PM System does not mean they are not important. While it is essential to measure progress and change throughout the health department, not all information should be included in the PM System. Everything that an agency does should not be included in the PM System. It would make the system too overwhelming to update and use. It is also important to focus on measuring impacts and changes to population health outcomes as a result of *programs and services*, not everyday tasks and/or projects. Project implementation for initiatives throughout the agency should not be monitored in the PM System. It is important to note that performance management (PM) should not be confused with project management. PM is the monitoring of meaningful initiatives and strategies that

GOAL 4 Strong Agency Infrastructure	Progress					
	Target	Period One	Period Two	Period Three	Period Four	Trend
Objective 1: Increase Workforce Support Structure						
Measures:						
Percent of employees who complete new employee orientation within 90 days	90	60	50	75	90	
Percent of employees reporting action on individual development plans	50	10	20	30	60	
# of initiatives implemented in the agency workforce development plan	3	1	2	3	4	

Figure 5.2 Example Performance Dashboard with Targets and Sparklines.

demonstrate agency value and outcomes. The purpose of measuring is not only to know how the organization is performing – but to enable it to perform better.

For example, with an immunization program a goal may be to monitor compliance among children with the immunization schedule prior to entering K-12. As a result of administering vaccines, ultimately the outcome of zero preventable disease outbreaks would be desirable. If a public health agency is struggling with immunization compliance (currently 73 percent compliant) due to resistance among the community, the public health agency may start to see vaccine-preventable outbreaks occur within the community that could have been prevented with increased vaccine compliance. The public health agency may then start to change their outreach efforts and educational materials related to vaccines in an effort to increase compliance rates to at least 90 percent in the next 12 months. Hypothetically, the agency tries something new and offers town-hall events. The Epidemiologist and Health Officer host the events and discuss the importance of vaccines, herd immunity, evidence-based practices and statistics, as well as potential public health risks if the community is not compliant with the recommended vaccine schedule. As a result of new programmatic efforts and continuous monitoring of the PM System, the immunization compliance rate increased from 73 percent to 81 percent after 6 months. The PM System helped the agency to determine that new programmatic efforts were successful in helping to make progress toward their goal. Based on this information, if the agency continues to offer the town-hall events in additional areas of the county (or state), they could continue to increase the immunization compliance rate until the goal is met.

While immunization compliance rates are an important and valuable performance measure to monitor, not all programmatic functions may be a priority-measure for the PM System. As an example, let's look at functions within Vital Statistics. Vital Statistics within a public health agency is crucial to understanding the population served. Data that is collected and monitored is often used to report on a state or county's population health status, life expectancy, infant mortality, etc. Another function of Vital Statistics may be to print birth certificates. While this is an important function and a needed-service for the community, measuring the number of birth certificates printed each month in the PM System is not necessarily a *meaningful* performance measure that demonstrates *impact* for the program or the agency. Printing birth certificates is a function that is considered a daily business function, business as usual. As long as the health department is open, this service will be offered. It does not mean that the function is not important or imperative, it is simply not a measure that demonstrates the impact of a program, service or operational process. However, Vital Statistics could include performance measures in the PM System to demonstrate effectiveness in meeting customer service needs. Remember, the members of the community are our customers and without them, public health services would not be needed. Public health agencies need to keep customer needs and their expectations in mind when implementing and monitoring programs and services.

As an example, perhaps the customers from the community often complain about the wait time to receive a birth certificate. The Vital Statistics area begins to monitor customer wait times in the PM System to establish a baseline and discovers that wait times for the month were, on average, 43 minutes per customer. As a result, a small team within Vital Statistics meets and uses Quality Improvement (QI) tools to determine what steps within the current process could be altered to make the process more efficient and decrease customer wait times. The team decides to cross-train staff to allow additional staff members the ability to serve customers who walk-in for services. One month after cross-training occurs, the average wait time has decreased to 14 minutes. The team reconvenes to discuss what else could be causing the delayed wait times and decides to offer a customer-experience survey in the lobby to obtain additional feedback. After administering the survey for 6 weeks, the team reviews the results and notices a recommendation that was suggested multiple times – to have the necessary forms online for customers to print out and complete prior to coming to the agency. The Vital Statistics program makes the following changes:

1 Posts the forms online in electronic format
2 Promotes that the forms are available online on their web page
3 Displays a flier in the lobby with the web information
4 Employees tell all customers that call in with inquiries related to printable birth and death certificates that forms can be filled out online prior to coming to decrease wait time

The PM System continues to show a decrease in the average customer wait time and after 8 months, it begins to hold steady at an average wait time of 7 minutes. Even though the program regularly monitored customer wait times in the PM System and was able to improve the wait time, it is important to continue monitoring this measure within the PM System on a monthly basis after the goal has been met. If after a year or more, the wait times begin to increase again, the program knows within a month (because measures are being updated monthly) that there is a potential problem and is able to revisit the process to see if additional changes should be made. Ultimately, customer service should be a priority for every public health agency. Customer service and experience should be monitored to some degree in all PM Systems.

Below is an example that walks through building out performance measures for the example discussed with Vital Statistics. As shown, the goal (high level umbrella statement) for Vital Statistics was to focus on providing

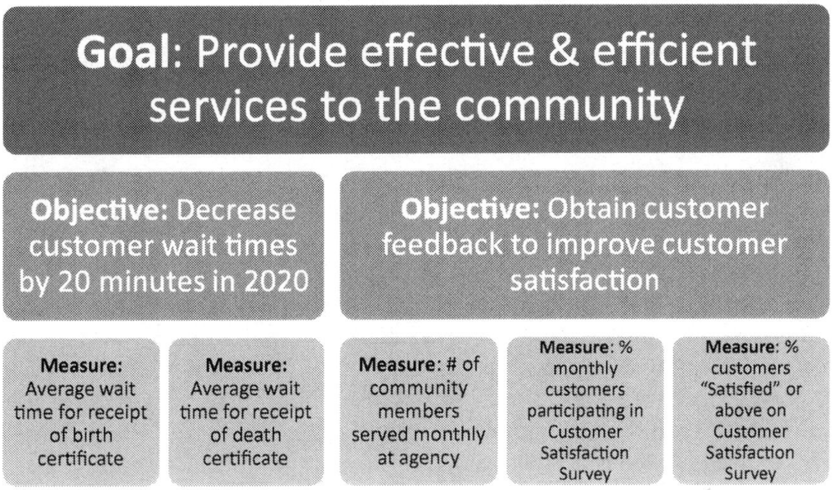

Goal: Provide effective & efficient services to the community

Objective: Decrease customer wait times by 20 minutes in 2020

Objective: Obtain customer feedback to improve customer satisfaction

Measure: Average wait time for receipt of birth certificate

Measure: Average wait time for receipt of death certificate

Measure: # of community members served monthly at agency

Measure: % monthly customers participating in Customer Satisfaction Survey

Measure: % customers "Satisfied" or above on Customer Satisfaction Survey

Figure 5.3 Example Programmatic Component in PM System – Vital Statistics.

effective and efficient services to the community they serve. That goal is then broken down into two objectives defining desired outcomes of decreasing customer wait times and using customer satisfaction data to improve processes within the program to ultimately improve customer satisfaction. A blank template has also been provided in the appendices that can be used during group discussion to guide the development of draft goals, objectives and measures. An example of the completed template is also provided as a tool in the appendices.

Strategic Plan Performance Measures

A strategic plan is a working document that allows agencies to focus on key public health priority areas with the central theme emphasizing the agency's vision and mission. Strategic plan priorities will differ for each health department and are typically updated every 3–5 years. Priorities for the strategic plan are often determined by a team within the health department, a leadership or management team, not one individual. Strategic planning cannot be done in a vacuum. Similar to PM, the strategic plan should not be used for implementing typical programmatic projects or monitoring business as usual activities. The strategic plan captures areas of focus for the health department and demonstrates to employees and the community what is currently inherent in the public health agency's operations. Priority areas of focus in the strategic plan may also include priorities identified in a health improvement plan. The public health agency exists to serve the needs of the community and when those needs are identified, plans to adjust and meet those needs should be done at the agency level, not just at the individual programmatic level. Incorporating areas of focus from an agency's health improvement plan into the strategic plan makes sense and allows for integration of operations within the agency. The strategic areas of focus should then trickle down to programs or divisions within the agency, also impacting their operational plans. Ideally, all divisions, programs and employees should be aware of the strategic plan priorities, their importance and understand how their program and position contribute to the success of the strategic plan.

During the development of the strategic plan, just as with public health programs, it is imperative to develop performance measures to monitor the progress and success of the strategic plan. Any public health agency can develop a strategic map, or strategic plan, but if it is not being implemented and monitored on a regular basis, the agency will likely not stay focused. Not all activities within strategic plan implementation/operational plans need to be included in the PM System. However, meaningful measures that are demonstrating impact should be included. An agency will likely not be working on addressing all priorities identified within the strategic plan at one time or within the same year. It is recommended to only include initiatives that are currently being worked on in the PM System for that year.

Figure 5.4 below shows an example goal included in an agency's strategic plan aimed at supporting a competent workforce. It is common for strategic planning goals to include workforce development priorities as workforce development planning efforts are recommended by the Public Health Accreditation Board.

Figure 5.4 Example Strategic Plan Performance Measures – Workforce Workgroup Specific.

- PHAB Measure 8.2.1: Maintain, implement and assess the health department workforce development plan that addresses the training needs of the staff and the development of core competencies; improve workforce development by identifying and addressing gaps in competence
- PHAB Measure 8.2.2: Maintain a competent health department workforce
- PHAB Measure 8.2.3: Provide professional and career development for all staff
- PHAB Measure 8.2.4: Establish policies that provide a work environment that is supportive to the workforce

It would not be expected for any agency to implement activities to support the above measures all at once. Rather, assess current workforce development efforts, strengths and gaps, and determine what can be implemented to support the strategic planning priority related to a competent workforce. In the example below the objective is to increase workforce support structure to improve engagement, to ultimately support a competent workforce. Some of the activities currently in place or being implemented in the short term include developing agency policies and standard operating procedures to support workforce development, implementing activities outlined in the workforce development plan and encouraging leadership to support increasing engagement among employees.

Health Improvement Plan Performance Measures

Health Improvement Plan priorities are typically dependent on the results of the state or local public health system assessment, with the essential services for public health at the foundation. The system assessment helps to gather information on public health programs and services currently available, identify gaps in care and services, and overall, identify the needs for the population being served. As a public health agency, these identified needs should set precedence for shifting capacity and programmatic resources – making them planning priorities. An example State Health Improvement Plan (SHIP) priorities can be seen in Figure 5.5.

The example SHIP has three priority areas and three cross-cutting areas of focus:

A Obesity
B Tobacco
C Behavioral Health
D Preventable Care and Avoidable Costs
E Data/Measurable Outcomes
F Community Engagement, Collaboration and Infrastructure

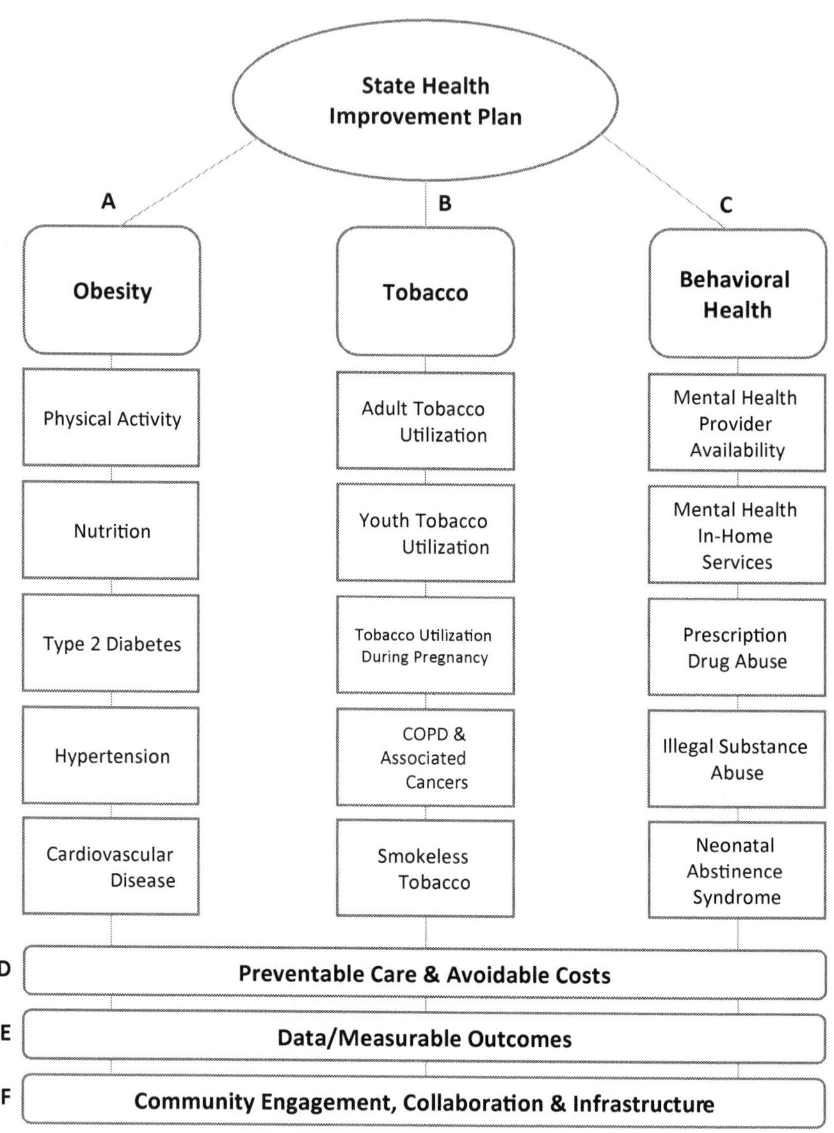

Figure 5.5 West Virginia State Health Improvement Plan Priorities.

Within the United States, health improvement plans and population health plans may focus on some of the same health factors such as obesity, tobacco, hypertension, cardiovascular disease and mental health. While priority areas may be similar across population health plans, the interventions being implemented will likely be different and unique to the community being served. Monitoring progress of activities that align with priorities of the SHIP/CHIP is essential to success. While a program may feel that their strategies and services will improve the population's health with regard to obesity, tobacco use and behavioral health issues, they will never be certain that they are making an impact if outcomes are not measured. It is within the strategies, interventions and programs in place that the performance measures will be derived. Again, performance measures should provide meaningful information that can be used to guide decision making. This would not include how many brochures are distributed related to tobacco programs – while that would tell us how many brochures are being distributed and printing budget needs, it does not give an accurate estimate on program engagement.

It is imperative to identify meaningful performance measures that will provide value-added information on program performance. Performance measures should provide feedback and allow the continuous monitoring of progress. Measuring the number of calls to the quit line will provide how many calls are being answered, but it does not provide the number of community members we are engaging. One member could be calling ten times per week, therefore we would not want to assume that all calls were unique

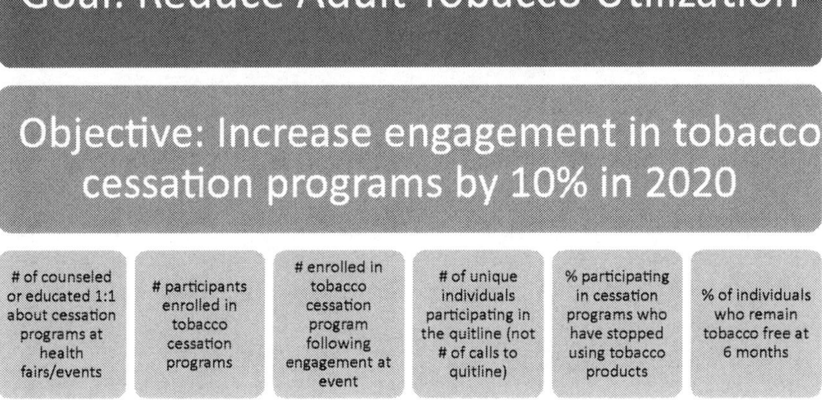

Figure 5.6 Example HIP Component within PM System.

participants. It is important to keep this mindset when determining which performance measures would be most useful in demonstrating programmatic reach, engagement and outcomes, regardless of the program.

In previous discussion we have looked at programmatic examples, administrative level strategic plan examples and population level – SHIP/CHIP measures. Measures related to the workforce development plan should also be included in the PM System and should be focused on the public health agency's workforce.

Workforce Development Plan Performance Measures

Public health agencies have the responsibility to provide the Essential Services of Public Health. In order to have the capacity to provide public health services to communities, public health agencies must have a competent public health workforce. Public health employees need to be proficient in the Core Competencies for Public Health Professionals in order to provide the essential services effectively and efficiently. This example takes a deeper dive into the Workforce Development Plan (WDP) compared to the previous strategic planning example related to the strategic priority focused on supporting efforts to maintain a competent workforce.

Workforce development planning (WDP)_usually starts with an assessment of the workforce. A WDP is often used to implement targeted activities in an agency to improve the public health workforce in areas that have been identified as part of a workforce assessment. Components may include:

- Training on Core Competencies for Public Health Professionals
- Succession and Retention
- Maintaining a Competent, Sustainable Workforce
- Professional Development
- Updating/Enhancing Job Descriptions to include applicable Core Competencies

Similar to the overall strategic plan, the WDP should have priority areas of focus but will also have operational plans that include 2–3 years of activities geared at improving the workforce. As the agency implements the WDP, developing performance measures that will allow the agency to monitor progress of the WDP will be crucial to success. These measures will also be a part of the PM System. An example of building WDP measures within the PM System is provided in Figure 5.7. One of the goals in the WDP is to ensure a competent public health workforce. A strategy to help meet that goal is to increase public health core competency abilities among staff. To help meet that objective, activities being implemented include conducting a workforce assessment against the core competencies for public health

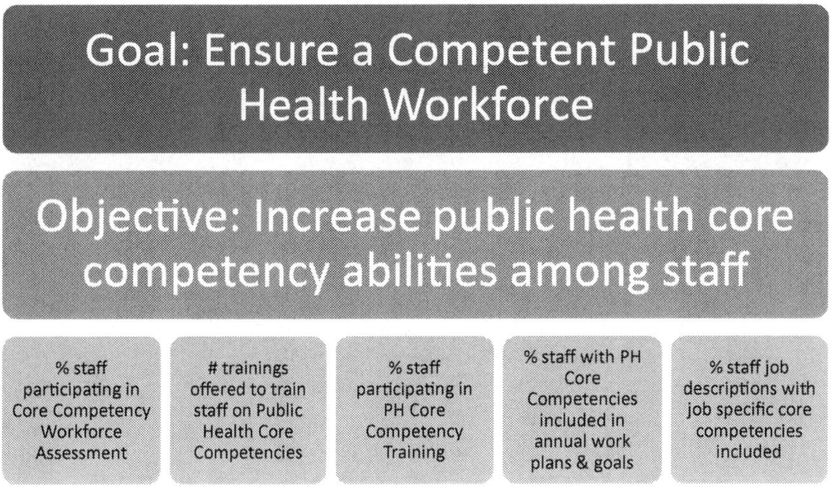

Goal: Ensure a Competent Public Health Workforce

Objective: Increase public health core competency abilities among staff

% staff participating in Core Competency Workforce Assessment

trainings offered to train staff on Public Health Core Competencies

% staff participating in PH Core Competency Training

% staff with PH Core Competencies included in annual work plans & goals

% staff job descriptions with job specific core competencies included

Figure 5.7 Example Workforce Development Component within PM System.

professionals, training staff on the core competencies, as well as encouraging managers and supervisors to include the core competencies in employee work plans and annual goals.

What Should Not be Included as Performance Measures?

The unique nature of every public health agency makes it difficult to name specific dos and don'ts. However, the key thing to keep in mind is that most PM System measures are monitoring activity over time. The data is supposed to provide just-in-time decision-making power. Reflect back to the speedometer and gas gauge examples from an actual car dashboard. These are monitored with intent because there are so many things riding on them; the consequences for speeding and running out of gas have been experienced by many, and efforts to avoid those consequences include careful monitoring of the dashboard. So, when selecting objectives, measures and targets, choose measures that need to be monitored over time. The PM System is not the only project management tool available to the agency. Completing installation of a new software system or an upgrade to facilities (new roof, tiling the halls) are both examples of important efforts to be monitored through careful project management, but they may not produce inputs that vary over time. Whereas an agency hoping to elevate their social media presence might need to consistently monitor social media posting numbers and engagement data to determine what is working and what can be improved. Therefore, as a basic guide, choose measures in the PM System that vary over time rather than one-and-done projects.

Tips and Techniques for Monitoring

This chapter provides several lists of questions, and this section continues the trend. The intention is to prepare performance managers with tools to lead effective processes and teams. Once goals, objectives, measures and targets have been selected, a process for monitoring must be developed. Most agencies develop a PM team (as required by PHAB), and sometimes that team is one of the existing leadership teams, or a combination of those teams.

Role Clarity: When the Performance Management Team (PMT) has been selected, role clarity is important.

1 Who will do the work of collecting the performance measures data on the frequency agreed upon?
2 Who will manage that process?
3 Who will do the reporting to the key audiences?
4 Why do these organizations/individuals have a vested interest in the success of the PM System?
5 How will the team review the data?

Successful teams answer these questions and have a written plan or procedure for managing the performance data collection process.

PMT Action: When the team convenes to review data, there may be many indicators to review. When the team meets, everyone should be able to see the data, therefore, restating the data can lead to dreadful meetings. Instead, effective PMTs often choose two to three questions for discussion at the PMT meeting for the measures that are doing well or struggling including but not limited to:

- Why do these data matter?
- What result do they produce?
- Is this the result the public/stakeholders are seeking?
- What partners were engaged in this work?
- Are additional partners needed for success?
- What opportunities exist to collaborate within the agency?
- How has this effort contributed to Public Health evidence base/research?
- What QI work is happening related to this measure?

The PMT should celebrate success and know they've accomplished their purpose when: (1) measures selected use the most appropriate variable; (2) results are relevant; (3) the data collection method is sound; (4) there is a well-written protocol; and (5) the reporting is accurate, precise, reproducible, fast and cost-effective.

Conclusion

Each of the areas described in this chapter could have their own dedicated publication on the intricacies of how to establish and implement a PM System. The goal should be to focus on priority information from each to develop a comprehensive and meaningful PM System. Using information from varying agency plans and initiatives (strategic plan, workforce development plan, public health programs) is a great way to begin the development of a comprehensive PM System. It can be difficult differentiating between project management vs. performance management and employee performance/evaluations vs. performance management. PM, when done correctly, is truly a representation of how the agency and/or program is performing, not how the individual employee is performing. A public health agency is a part of the state's health care system and has the ability to shift focus, program capacity and resources, to improve to the best of their ability. As priorities change within the community, as health priorities change from one community health assessment to the next and as priorities change with regard to the workforce, priorities should also change within the public health agency. Documenting these priorities in one location, the PM System and updating on a regular basis is an efficient and effective way of monitoring all agency programs, plans and progress being made.

References and Resources

1 Covey, S. R. (1989). *Seven Habits of Highly Effective.* New York, NY: Free Press, a Div. of Simon and Schuster.

2 Public Health Accreditation Board. (2013, December). *PHAB Standards and Measures, Version 1.5.* Retrieved 2019, from www.phaboard.org: www.phaboard.org/wp-content/uploads/SM-Version-1.5-Board-adopted-FINAL-01-24-2014.docx.pdf

3 Lichiello, P. (n.d.). *Guidebook for Performance Measurement.* Retrieved from Public Health Foundation: www.phf.org/resourcestools/Documents/PMCguidebook.pdf

6 Implementation and Maintenance of a Performance Management System

In a Performance Management System (PM System), the goal is to use measured performance information systematically, and repeatedly, through a regular cycle of decision making in an attempt to keep managing and improving future performance. Upon initial planning, PM System implementation should be looked at from a big-picture, strategic standpoint. Performance Management (PM) allows agencies to consider how all programs within the agency all work together to provide essential public health services to the community served. Consider larger initiatives or plans that impact the entire agency – strategic plan, workforce development plan, community health assessments, health improvement plans, accreditation readiness, operational plans, etc. These plans also need to be incorporated into the PM System, to some degree.

PDCA in Performance Management

Think back to a time when peers worked together to plan, set expectations, collect information regarding progress toward achieving those expectations, and then used that information to set the direction for next steps. This is the same process utilized for PM, just on a bigger scale. It is also similar to the Plan Do Check Act (PDCA) Cycle used in quality improvement (QI) planning (refer to Figure 6.1). Notice that this is a continuous cycle. The model also includes the elements of the Turning Point framework. There are multiple time frames going on here. Performance measures and performance standards including goals and targets are reflected in both the multi-year and annual plans.

Keep in mind, start where the agency is now. It's completely okay to just be starting out with implementation, just as it is ok to be two years into your PM System and realize that it's not providing the information needed. In fact, agencies who are successful in this work report that "It may take a couple of planning cycles to get everything working together in a smooth fashion."[5] Start with the planning phase. Initially, the majority of time and effort will be spent in the "Planning" stage developing draft components of the plan – from

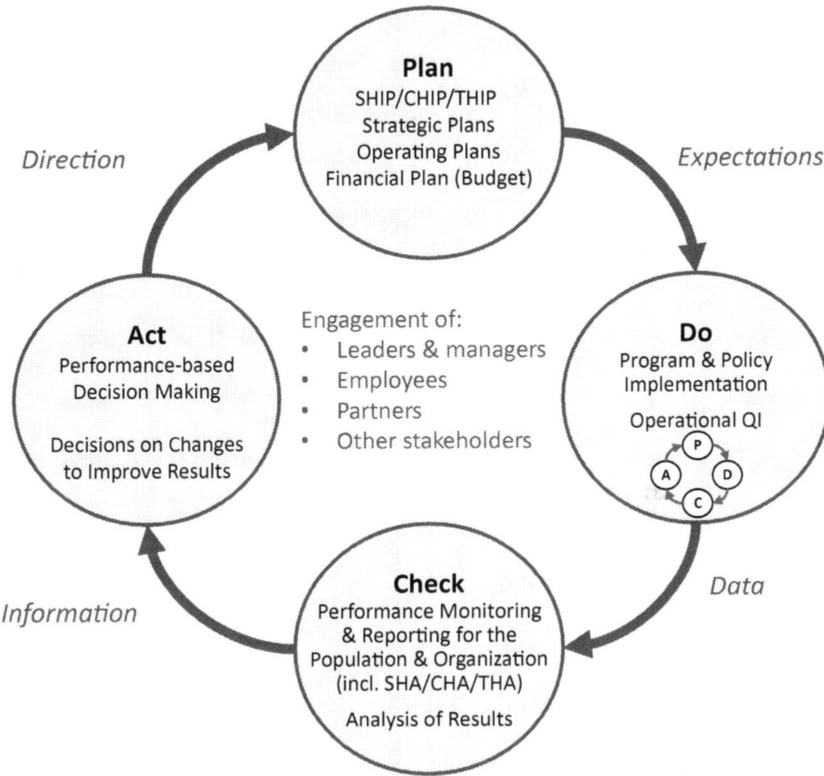

Figure 6.1 QI Framework for a Public Health Organization-wide PM System.

individual programs to agency-wide initiatives and plans. Keep in mind that, while it is important to plan well, because of the cyclical nature of this cycle, components of the PM System do not have to be perfect in the beginning. Evaluate information that is available to help determine priority areas of focus. Does the agency have a Health Improvement Plan? If so, include performance measures related to progress on the health improvement plan. If no health improvement plan exists, consider integrating these plans in the future. Start with the assessment process and work toward identifying health improvement plan priorities over the next year. Once that is complete, then incorporate those priorities into the PM System. The cycle is continuous; what is learned in one cycle informs decisions and plans for the next cycle. For example, the health assessment is in the Check stage, which means it will provide assessment information for the health improvement plan that follows in the Plan stage the next time we go through the cycle.

Does the agency have a Strategic Plan? If not, just as above, incorporate working toward creating a strategic plan over the next 1–2 years and then include measures in the PM System. If a strategic plan exists, and it is current, identify the top priorities of the plan and include in the PM System. A few existing programs or services may be considered particularly important or "strategic" to improve. With regards to Financial Plan or Budget being included in the "Planning" stage, agency priorities should drive the budget. The budget should not drive priorities. Sometimes additional funds may be budgeted to increase performance of those strategic programs. Whether or not additional funds are available, those strategic programs or services can be considered likely candidates for focused QI efforts. Therefore, "Operational QI" is shown as part of the "Do" stage. "Operational QI" is a short-term improvement cycle occurring within the overall improvement cycle of the PM System. The PM System is being used as a guide to improve organizational processes – it is large scale, usually working in annual or multi-year time-frames. Operational level QI is occurring as frequently as collecting and analyzing data – for some programs that may be weekly or monthly.

Quality is more important than the quantity of measures. Start with a few meaningful measures for each program and for each of the agency-wide plans, begin to monitor them and use the data you collect to guide decision making and improve for the next cycle. Managers and staff of all programs can be challenged to apply QI techniques to their operations to improve measurable performance beyond the targets in their operating plan.

When combining the PDCA model with the Turning Point Model discussed in Chapter 2, it becomes evident how PM and QI work together.

Setting expectations, developing standards, setting goals and targets occurs in the "Planning" stage. The "Do" stage is where program implementation happens – operationalizing strategic plans, workforce development plans, the day-to-day operations within individual programs, etc. As we begin to collect data on the performance measures related to these activities through regular reporting of progress and sharing of information, we are entering the "Check" phase. Next, the process of monitoring this information, analyzing and interpreting the results. Is the program doing well? Is the program performing as anticipated? Use information from the "Check" phase to inform the "Act" stage of the cycle. The process of collecting and analyzing the data from the PM System does not improve performance on its own. Someone must act on the information, use it to fine tune processes or implement new strategies that will lead to better performance. If data from the PM System demonstrates that the program is performing as expected and meeting goals, stay on course. If not, use this data to dive a little deeper into the program/plan and determine what needs to change or improve to drive better outcomes. This particular area is often where individual QI projects come out of the PM System. Through the process of collecting data, analyzing and interpreting the results

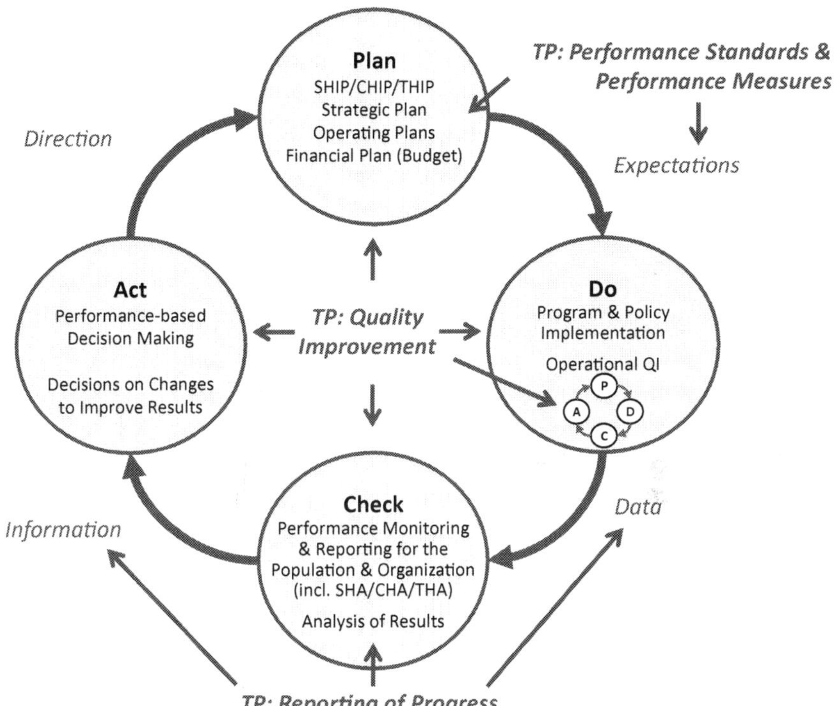

Figure 6.2 QI Framework for a PH PM System Including All Four Turning Point Quadrants.

is how the need for improvement efforts are recognized. When results are not as anticipated, focus in on the strategies in place to determine what gaps exist in the process, what are the root causes driving this process to not perform as anticipated and what solutions can be implemented to see if a positive impact is made on the data. View the PM System as your telescope and QI as your microscope. The PM System is providing a big picture view while utilizing QI tools to fine tune processes that will impact big picture results. The information collected during the "Check" phase and implemented during the "Act" phase will then provide direction in the next planning stage for the continuous PDCA cycle.

Key Elements of Successful PM Systems

This section builds on concepts introduced in Chapter 2. Successful implementation of the PM System includes these key elements.

1 Leadership engagement
2 Employee engagement
3 PM System Design Team
4 Reporting
5 PM/QI Council or Team
6 Communication
7 Sustaining the Process

Leadership Engagement

Senior leadership must communicate the need, importance and expectations related to the PM System. It is also necessary that leadership designate the resources. Financial resources are nearly always needed for training or coaching to develop and design the process. Some organizations find that software or web-based systems support this action and those require financial resources. The most important resource is the allocation of staff time for the implementation and maintenance of the PM System. Organizations need strategies to assure that PM is active and integrated into regular operations. One strategy to keep leadership engaged with PM is to create a standing agenda item on regular leadership team meetings. This concept of visible leadership is defined in the Public Health Performance Management Self-Assessment Tool which begins framing visible leadership as: "Senior management commitment to a culture of quality that aligns PM practices with the organizational mission, regularly takes into account customer feedback, and enables transparency about performance between leadership and staff."[1] This idea is reinforced by a *Performance Management Leadership Guide* created by the Association of State and Territorial Health Officials which states: "Building a useful PM system requires a full commitment from the executive team. Your vision for the system should be clearly and frequently articulated."[2] Investing in staff training is critical to successfully deploy a PM process. Senior leaders must be visible in those regular training events to lend credibility and social capital to the importance of the process.

Employee Engagement

The Performance Management Self-Assessment suggests through the assessment questions several strategies for engaging staff. Training is the first step. Understanding the value of PM is not immediately obvious to everyone. PM skills – like designing effective measures or monitoring progress on objectives – are not part of the academic preparation for most public health and health care workforce members. Participation in training builds competence and confidence. There are additional benefits for engaging all employees in the PM process. A study in the *Journal of Organizational Behavior* reported on drivers of workforce engagement and among their "results reveal that the primary driver of workforce engagement in work is a work context where people experience the organization as being goal directed and demonstrating concern for people."[3] Employees want to know what the goals are and how they contribute. There are opportunities to engage employees at different organizational levels and in levels of investment of time throughout these remaining key elements.

PM System Design Team

The development of a PM System is usually led by a design team; this is a team of individuals designated by leadership. The design team has clear ownership of the PM System and should consist of at least one member in a leadership, authoritative role. The design team is responsible for defining the PM framework. A good place to start is by discussing and defining the following:

- Purpose – what is the purpose of the PM System? What do we want it to do today and in the future?
- Functional requirements – what is it supposed to do?
- Performance requirements – how will the system perform its function?
- Usability requirements – who are the users and what do they need from the system?
- Data semantics – define the key business and process terminology that will be used
- Budget – determine ongoing staffing, licensing, operation and upgrade costs

Agencies need a clear roadmap for how to begin, and the Action Plan outlined in Figure 6.3 can provide those key first steps. Agencies vary, so there may be additional steps needed for procedural differences, but these are the basic steps for beginning. One way that agencies stumble in their PM System Implementation is to skip this design team step. Making the leap from a desire to have a PM System to the gathering of the PM/QI Team can lead to confusion and this slows the process.

After the pilot phase, design team should work with programs throughout the agency and with members of the leadership team to determine the best approach for implementing the PM System. Take into consideration the capacity of the agency and programs. Available resources will vary drastically from a small health department with a handful of employees to a large agency with more than 500 employees. While PM Systems are not one-size fits all, this approach will work well for most programs within the agency.

Action Plan for the PM System Design Team				
Major Action Steps (What will be done)	**Lead Person (by whom)**	**Target Date**	**Revised Date**	**Actual Date**
1. Identify Design Team & Team Leader				
2. Identify key stakeholders & the process to engage them				
3. Adopt an approach to tracking and reporting (spreadsheets, software, including reporting periods)				
4. Select pilot groups (e.g. programs or divisions) to test the system				
5. Pilot groups develops PMS with goals, objectives, measures & targets				
6. Pilot group tests the PMS for one or two reporting periods				
7. Stakeholders review and improve pilot PMS				
8. Revise Tools (spreadsheets, data collection systems) and develop user guidance based on review of pilot				
9. Plan further system implementation - rollout to other departments				

Figure 6.3 Action Plan for the PM System Design Team.

PM System Design Team should meet regularly (at least monthly). This team will be responsible for:

- Making decisions on operational guidance, software, reporting format and frequency (see Figure 6.3)
- Determining IT needs and support
- Working with programs throughout the agency (as needed) to develop meaningful goals, objectives and performance measures to be included in the PM System
- Guiding deployment throughout the organization, providing varying levels of support based on program needs
- Obtaining feedback from leadership, programs and users to ensure the system is meeting anticipated needs
- Tweaks to the process and system to allow for continuous improvement

Once the PM System framework is designed and ready for implementation, the design team can transition to the PM/QI Team.

Reporting

Once measures have been adopted by programs (Step 5 of Major Action Steps in Figure 6.3), the implementation begins. The PM System needs to capture the performance data. It would be nice if agencies had all data necessary in one cohesive system where software could automatically query and populate the tracking spreadsheets. In the absence of that kind of technology (which would be akin to finding a unicorn), a process is needed and these questions are intended to help design teams build the system that makes sense for the unique needs of each agency.

Time: What is the time frame for reporting? Is the system collecting data weekly (rare) monthly or quarterly? What is the lag time? For example, if the plan is to use quarterly data, and the quarter ends March 31, what is a reasonable expectation for timely reporting? Can data be clean and accurate by April 15? This is important because it influences the timing of the convening of the PM/QI Team. This table provides a potential time frame for organizations that adopt quarterly reporting.

Responsible Party: In each program, a person needs to be designated as the responsible party for entering the data. The accountability for data collection and entering must be at the program level and not the sole responsibility of the performance improvement manager.

PM/QI Council

So much energy, design, staff time and training goes in to developing the PM System, and then the task turns to actually using the system. Again, the *Performance Management Self-Assessment*[1] can serve as a reminder about what needs to be done; agencies are expected to use performance data to do the following:

A Determine areas for more analysis or evaluation
B Set priorities and allocate/redirect resources
C Inform policy makers of the observed or potential impact of decisions under their consideration
D Implement QI projects
E Make changes to improve performance and outcomes
F Improve performance

This list of expectations helps clarify the purpose of the PM/QI Council.

Table 6.1 Example PM Data Quarterly Reporting Deadlines

Data Reporting Time Frame	*Deadline for Data Reporting*	*Date of PM/QI Team Meeting*
January–March	April 15	First week of May
April–June	July 15	First week of August
July–September	October 15	First week of November
October–December	January 15	First week of February

There are many approaches to how that work actually gets done. Some agencies will have separate teams or councils for PM and QI, and some combine the two. If resources allow, once the PM System is fully functional, it may be more effective to have one team focused on both PM and QI.

The PM/QI Council should be striving to assure that (1) measures selected use the most appropriate variable, (2) results are relevant, (3) the data collection method is sound and (4) that the reporting is accurate, precise, reproducible, fast and cost-effective. When all of those conditions are achieved, then the Council can decide what discussion and deliberation questions would be most beneficial to help the programs/agency improve performance. Example discussion questions were proposed in Chapter 5.

The PM/QI Council should determine PM System implementation steps together. It is best to do this in a brainstorming session with each member sharing thoughts on steps that should occur from planning to implementation, and maintenance. One strategy is to create a simple table in Word or Excel to organize agreed upon action items (similar to Figure 6.3). Always include columns to assign *task responsibility* and *time frames* to build in accountability.

Communication Strategy

The communication strategy helps define the success of a PM System. It can help gain support, staff time and momentum. There are three distinct phases to implementing an organizational-wide PM System – development, deployment and sustainment. Each phase may involve different people and therefore communications may need to be tailored depending on the particular audience.

Development Phase

The Design Team should consider message design right from the start. Questions to ask in the development phase include:

- What are we trying to achieve by deploying a PM System?
- Accreditation, increasing awareness, changing audience behavior, etc.
- What do we want our audience to think after learning about the PM System?
- What does our audience think now? What are their greatest needs and challenges?
- What is the connection between this project and other programs work?
- What other PM Systems or activities exist in the agency already?
- Are they working? Can they be leveraged?
- What behavior or actions do we need from our audience?
- Participation in the development, time, expertise, support, promotion

Deployment

The Design Team may also be managing communication during the initial deployment phase. Questions that may shape the messaging related to deployment of the PM System include:

- What are we trying to achieve in the deployment stage?
    - Increasing awareness, action, involvement, changing audience behavior, etc.
- What do we want our audience to know during this phase?
    - What does our audience know now?
    - What are their greatest needs and challenges during this phase?
    - What is in it for them? How does this help them?
- What do we want our audience to do during this phase?
    - Do we need their support? Are there steps they need to take?
    - What are the key milestones that impact our audience?

Sustainment

In this phase, it may be possible to pass the baton from the Design Team to the PM/QI Council as now the team should have stories to tell. Questions that may shape the messaging related to sustainment of the PM System include:

- How has PM resulted in improvements? Tangible results?
- What is the connection between PM/QI successes and other programs?
- What do we want our audience to do during this phase?
- Are there steps they need to take? What are the challenges they have?

Across all phases of the communication work, there are universal communication basics that will help assure success. First, who needs to care about performance improvement work? The audiences might be external, like annual report recipients, grant program officers, board members, coalitions and newsletter recipients; or the audiences may be internal, including all levels of staff. Framing of the messages must always consider why the audience should care – drawing connections to the values or issues that the message recipient is invested in. Messages about PM/QI need to be clear about what success mean, and this is usually provided through the measure targets. The PM System can help with both big-picture storytelling and specific storytelling. At a high level, it is helpful to be able to distill the PM System into a one page map. There are many ways to do this, and one example is included in Figure A.6 in the Appendix from The Georgia Department of Public Health.

For internal audiences, consider your many opportunities to share specific PM/QI stories through staff meetings, performance appraisals, email and newsletters, intranet or new employee orientation. At one agency, for every measure in the PM System, the program responsible for the measure created a line of sight connecting the measure → to the reason for the measure → to the mission for the agency. All measures were graphically designed and branded, and then every Wednesday for over a year, one measure would be selected and emailed to all staff to illustrate "Why we do what we do Wednesdays." Keeping this visible in the agency is critical to sustaining the work.

There are additional resources that may be useful to public health practitioners. NACCHO created a Guide to Communicating about Performance Improvement. NACCHO's description of the resource states:

> This easy-to-read guide is designed to help LHDs share their performance improvement stories with key audiences. The guide uses a step by step approach to help LHDs craft tailor-made messages and strategies to help build support and understanding of performance improvement with staff members before reaching out to governing bodies and the media.[4]

This resource is packed with additional case study examples of Performance Improvement communication strategies.

Like every other phase of this work, the communications strategy requires a plan. The Communication Plan can have varying levels of detail, but the best beginning starts with the basics which include the message, date to deploy, the audience, the channel or communication format and as always – most-importantly – who will lead that effort. This assumes that the work of messaging communication about performance improvement is shared across multiple people, and this is key to creating a culture of quality.

The PM/QI Council can also develop materials to promote their mission and vision with all employees throughout the agency. The example below is shared with us by the Wyoming Department of Health's Performance Management and Quality Improvement Council. This is a promotional document developed to share information about the Council and how they impact organizational culture. It also provides information to employees on the PM model from Wyoming DOH's perspective, training opportunities related to PM and QI for employees, as well as additional resources available through the department's intranet.

Message	Date	Audience	Communication format (email, meeting, newsletter, etc.)	Person Responsible

Figure 6.4 Communication Planning Template.

We exist

to systematically support PHD's active use of data to manage and improve program and division performance.

We do that by

- establishing, maintaining, and enhancing PHD's PM and QI infrastructure
- offering PM and QI coaching and support
- providing or sourcing PM and QI training opportunities
- developing, implementing, and monitoring PHD's PMQI Plan
- communicating and celebrating process and performance improvement

To achieve a culture that

- identifies and builds upon success and opportunities through performance management
- responds and adapts so we can provide the best services to improve health in Wyoming
- uses a sustainable framework for PM and QI efforts

How We Can Help

- Provide assistance in identifying meaningful goals, objectives, measures, and/or targets to monitor and manage performance.
- Offer support related to using PM data to tell a story of performance
- Provide coaching and support for QI projects
- Provide or source PMQI training opportunities
- Work with staff to disseminate QI successes and lessons learned
- Provide support to programs preparing for Division and/or Department HealthStat

Training & Support Opportunities

- New employee training offered quarterly
- Public speaking training and refreshers
- PMQIC Office Hours
- Online training options through WYTRAIN and other trusted public health training sources

* Training options may change as need and resources change.

Division HealthStat

Annual Division HealthStat meetings are scheduled to offer opportunities for programs to report on performance and improvement efforts, discuss successes and challenges, and provide learning and collaboration opportunities within PHD.

Learn More

Use the PHD Intranet to find more information about PM and QI, the council, and related tools and resources.

- https://sites.google.com/wyo.gov/wdh-intranet-phd/home/accreditation-for-now/performance-management
- https://sites.google.com/wyo.gov/wdh-intranet-phd/home/accreditation-for-now/quality-improvement

Request assistance: https://forms.gle/WSQi3twWSb9LHRKP6

For more information, contact: Feliciana Turner | Performance Improvement Manager | 307-777-8946 | feliciana.turner@wyo.gov

The Performance Management Model in Action

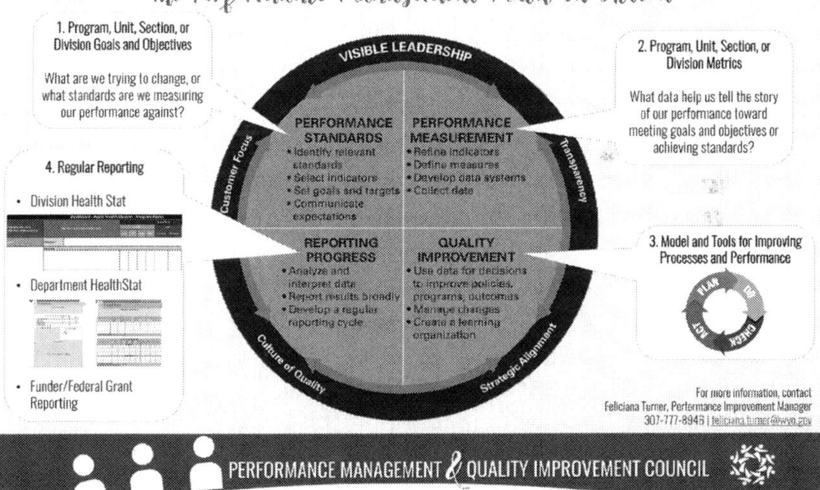

PERFORMANCE MANAGEMENT & QUALITY IMPROVEMENT COUNCIL
Public Health Division
Wyoming Department of Health

Figure 6.5 Wyoming Department of Health Performance Management and Quality Improvement Model.

continued

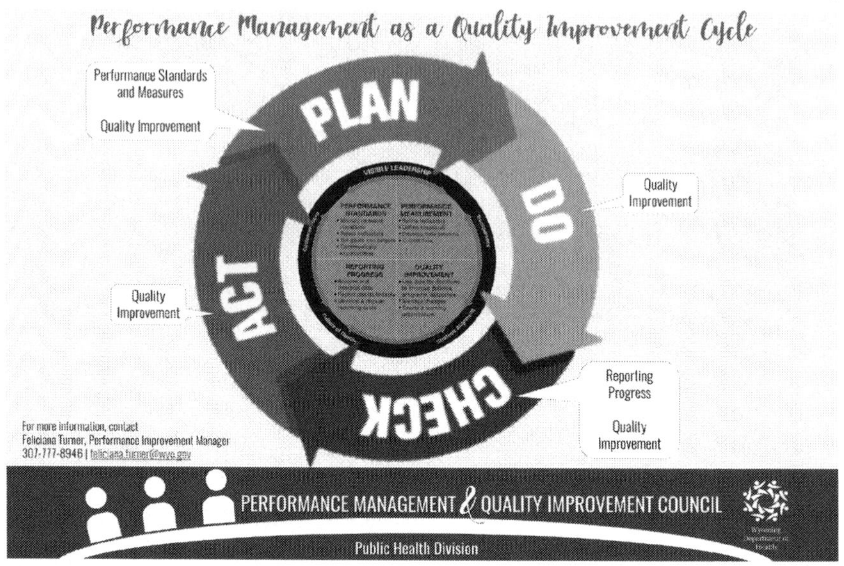

Figure 6.5 Continued

Sustainability Management

The first step in designing a sustainable system is to start small. Design a process that identifies a series of measures that assures that all departmental programmatic units feel represented, but also the agency system must include just the key metrics, not every single data point available. This is key to sustainability because systems that are too big create work, and then they create work avoidance and the systems fail. Consider this idea of PDCA for Sustainability. At a system level, consider what is emerging and whether everything is being done that can be done to achieve the objectives and goals. This is done through the PM/QI Council. Then, a performance improvement manager should meet, at least annually, with every program that contributes measures to the PM System. Those conversations can "check" to determine whether measures are being met, whether they tell a complete story and whether changes need to be made. Then, to sustain this process, assure that the communications plan is being implemented to celebrate the successes.

Conclusion

PM is easy to define; it is simply about using performance measurement information to make better decisions. Easy to define, not always easy to do.

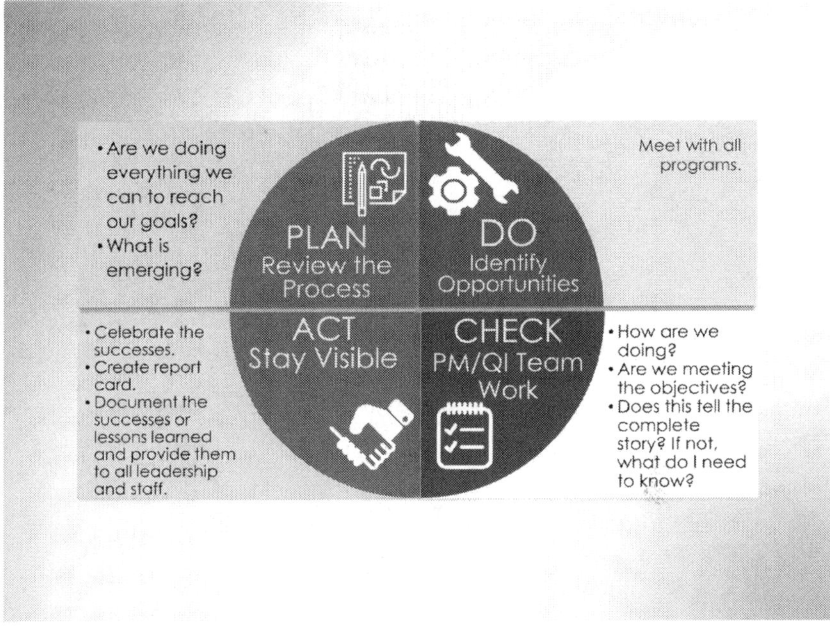

Figure 6.6 PDCA of Sustainability.

There are many lessons learned from working in the field with public health agencies:

1 No two agencies are the same – the size, number of employees, programs (number, types, organization, goals, funding), therefore, there is no model standard for the PM System.
2 Agencies get started with strategic planning, health assessments, health improvement plans and workforce development plans at a variety of time frames. There is no best order for beginning PM and QI planning; just start.
3 PM Systems – development, implementation, reporting, frequency, programmatic support – are as unique as the agency leading the work and those differences are appropriate.
4 Terminology is different from one agency to another. Different systems organize their staff hierarchies in a variety of ways like program, unit, office, division, department, agency, etc. Similarly, different PM Systems use different hierarchical language to organize the structure of the system, for example: priorities, goals, objectives, strategies, measures, key performance indicators, etc. Just choose the hierarchy that makes

sense to the organization. Public health agencies planning to pursue accreditation should take notice of the language listed in the Public Health Accreditation Board Standards and Measures, related to goals, objectives and measures.

5 Networks are important. Most work happens in teams, but the PM role at an agency is often one person. In PM/QI work, there are robust networks of colleagues who will share their best practices and experiences with failure. There is no need to face this work alone.

References and Resources

1 Public Health Foundation. (2013). *Performance Management Self-Assessment.* Retrieved from www.phf.org/focusareas/performancemanagement/toolkit/Pages/PM_Toolkit_Self_Assessment.aspx

2 Chapman, R. W. (2017). *Performance Management Leadership Guide. Performance Management Leadership Guide*. Association of State and Territorial Health Officials. Retrieved from www.astho.org/Accreditation-and-Performance/ASTHO-Performance-Management-Leadership-Guide/

3 Schneider, B., Yost, A. B., Kropp, A., Kind, C. and Lam, H. Workforce engagement: What it is, what drives it, and why it matters for organizational performance. *J Organ Behav*. 2018; 39: 462–480. https://doi-org.proxy.wichita.edu/10.1002/job.2244

4 National Association of County and City Health Officials. (2013). *Guide to Communicating about Performance Improvement. Guide to Communicating about Performance Improvement.* Retrieved from http://toolbox.naccho.org/pages/tool-view.html?id=3640&userToken=ad38f0da-ede6-4b7a-9f13-69ea31ad1b0f&Site=NACCHO

5 Mason, P. (2018). Clackamas County Public Health. Journal of Public Health Management and Practice, 24. doi: 10.1097/phh.0000000000000705

7 Developing a Performance Management Plan

Implementing performance management (PM) and tying to quality improvement (QI) efforts as well as strategic planning, health improvement planning or other large agency initiatives can seem like a daunting task. The chapters throughout this guide book have walked through where to begin, information gathering, assessing leadership support and organizational culture, as well as developing goals, objectives and measures. The next step is to create a Performance Management Plan (PM Plan). The written plan is fundamental to assuring that the Performance Management System (PM System) is sustained. PM, QI and health improvement planning efforts will differ in format, implementation, size and reporting from one agency to another, as will the PM Plan. The PM Plan will differ from one agency to another. Agencies will often combine their PM and QI efforts into one plan, developing a PM/QI Plan. Information included in the PM Plan will vary and can include, but would not be limited to:

- Purpose of the PM Plan (or PM/QI Plan)
- Definition of Performance Management and Quality Improvement
- Key Definitions
- Culture
- Support Structure
- PM Council (or PM/QI Council)
- Training and Resources
- Developing Goals, Objectives and Measures
- Procedure Steps
- Identifying Improvement Efforts
- Monitoring and Reporting
- Communication and Engagement
- Work Plan

Purpose

Use this section of the plan as an opportunity to describe why the plan was created and what it is intended to provide. The purpose might be to provide a framework for organizational PM and QI efforts, to align with other agency plans and initiatives or to introduce the foundation and structure in which the agency conducts PM activities. The Purpose statement will ultimately serve as a guide to support measuring performance and improving operations. This is also the area to discuss the agency's commitment to enhancing a culture of PM/QI and the desired impact. The purpose portion of the plan is typically 1–2 paragraphs.

Definition of PM

This section is often used to set the tone or create a consistent use of terminology. Describe what PM means to the agency and how it aligns with the agency's mission, vision and strategic goals. Outline key components to the PM System. Some agencies will also define components of the Turning Point Framework: PM standards, performance measures, the QI process, reporting of progress and what each of these mean as part of the agency's PM System.

Key Definitions

If the agency is adopting the Public Health Performance Management Model that has been referenced throughout this guidebook, then this section of the plan might include these definitions.

> **Performance Standards**: Organizational or system expectations to improve public health practices based on internal or external goals or benchmarks.
>
> **Performance Measures**: Clearly defined indicators for collecting data to assess achievement of standards.
>
> **Reporting of Progress**: Documenting and analyzing results vs. expectations and communicating such information as feedback to guide future performance improvement decisions.
>
> **Quality Improvement**: A process to manage change and improve performance in public health policies, programs or infrastructure based on standards, data and reports.

This section of the plan clarifies that hierarchy and how that is defined by the agency. Throughout the examples in this guidebook, the structure has been Goal>Objectives>Measures. Example definitions could be:

Goal: A goal is an abstract and general umbrella statement, under which specific objectives can be clustered. A goal is an overarching principle that guides decision making.

Objective: Objectives are statements that describe desired outcomes. Objectives are specific, measurable steps that can be taken to meet the goal.

Measures: There are many ways to define measures. For a good example of possible measures definitions, take a look at the example plan from New Mexico, available in Chapter 8.

Based on history and experience and current demands to align with other plans, all agencies choose a variety of ways to organize their hierarchy for aligning PM. While the examples throughout have been Goal>Objectives>Measures, other structures work as well. In the Appendix, Figure A.7, you will see an example from Portsmouth Virginia Public Health Department where their hierarchy is organized as strategy>objective>action. This is why the definitions section is important.

Additionally, if the plan is a combined QI and PM Plan, there are dozens of models of QI plans available that provide example definitions of QI terms. These typically include aim statements, several kinds of QI tools and PDCA. There are a number of great resources for finding definitions of the agency's priority terms like the *Public Health Quality Improvement Encyclopedia*,[1] *Embracing Quality in Public Health: A Practitioner's Quality Improvement Guidebook*,[2] or the ASQ Quality Glossary of Terms, Acronyms and Definitions.[3]

Culture

ASQ defines culture as "a common set of values, beliefs, attitudes, perceptions and accepted behaviors shared by individuals within an organization."[3] If you tolerate it, it is culture. This section clarifies the aspiration for the PM values and beliefs. When writing this section, look back at the characteristics of Stage 5, outlined in Chapter 4. Also, look ahead to Chapter 8 and see the example that New Mexico provides under "The Culture Behind The Strategic Planning Roadmap."

Support Structure

How will this work be staffed? Just as every plan is as unique as the agency creating it, the process for managing the PM System varies from agency to agency based on their own unique structures and where staff exhibit capacity and skills. This section makes clear the name of at least one position that has responsibility to implementation of this plan. This may also outline the expectations of leadership at the executive and program level to support the implementation of this process.

Council

The activities of the Council (or team) are described in Chapter 6. The PM Plan document needs to identify the participants by role and outline their function. Identifying a team to serve as the PM Review Council or Team is fundamental to the process. The PHAB Standards and Measures state that:

> The health department must provide documentation of a department committee, team, council, executive team, or some other entity that is responsible for implementing the performance management system. This does not have to be a separate group that deals only with performance management but may be a function of a standing department committee.[4]

There are many ways to structure this. Some organizations assign this responsibility to their leadership team and devote time in every meeting or every other meeting to review sections of the PM System. Some organizations convene all program managers quarterly to discuss the lessons learned and report out their PM data. This section of the PM Plan just makes that membership and responsibilities of the PM Council clear.

Training and Resources

Ensure that members of the Council receive sufficient training to carry out their responsibilities. Determine and describe in this section what resources will be made available to all employees within the agency to improve the performance and quality of programs and services. All training opportunities should be targeted to improve PM and QI skills, knowledge and practices. Assess the workforce to determine training needs and opportunities for improving knowledge and skills in this area. Assessment options can include the PM self assessment and assessing the workforce against the core competencies for public health professionals.

Consider offering a variety of training options for employees. Employees may be starting at different levels with regards to PM and improvement efforts. Perhaps this will be a new topic for some and a refresher course for others. Introductory trainings can be offered during new employee orientation to ensure that all employees are familiar with agency efforts to build and maintain a culture focused on performance and quality. Introducing employees to these concepts with a "hands-on," applicationbased approach can be done in a workshop setting where employees are learning about PM and QI tools as they apply them to specific scenarios within their programs. Plan for ongoing or annual trainings to members of the Council and/or all employees that focus on additional methods and tools needed for identifying and implementing improvement efforts, data collection, monitoring and reporting. A one-and-done approach – where agencies train once and expect systemic improvement – is a pitfall to be avoided. PM coaching can also be made available by the Council to employees who have identified an area that needs improvement but may be lacking the knowledge or tools to implement on their own.

Even though these trainings are focused more on QI and PM, they are still training the workforce. Coordinate training efforts with the workforce development plan or those responsible for planning workforce development efforts.

Developing Goals, Objectives and Measures

Chapter 5 provides a comprehensive overview of developing goals, objectives and measures. In the PM Plan, this section would define the steps programs within the agency would take to begin prioritizing and developing meaningful goals, and associated objectives and measures. If the Council is available as a resource to help programs build out this information, perhaps even with prioritizing goals, define that here. Make a plan for annual reviews of agency and programmatic goals, objectives and measures within the PM System. Once they are developed and included in the PM System, that does not necessarily mean they will always be a part of the system. A documented annual review of all goals, objectives and measures ensures that the PM System includes meaningful information and that information within does not become stagnant. Programs should also be required to review and update goals, objectives and measures within the PM System on an annual basis.

Identifying Improvement Efforts

The most meaningful part of any PM System is using the information within to guide decision making. The PM System provides information that allows processes within programs to improve outcomes, increase quality and therefore increase efficiency and overall effectiveness. Use the data being reported within the PM System to identify improvement efforts. If the Council is available to assist the agency and associated programs with utilizing PM System data to identify improvement efforts, outline the process for initiating that request.

Monitoring and Reporting

How will regular reporting be collected in the PM System? How will the data within be monitored? A standardized method for organizing all goals, objectives and measures within the PM System should be established prior to implementation. Within the PM Plan, discuss expectations for ongoing monitoring of the PM System, the Council's role, the utilization of the data throughout the agency. Performance measures should ideally be updated monthly or quarterly. Fewer measures should be updated bi-annually, and even fewer, annually. If a measure can only be tracked annually, how is this performance data helping the agency improve operations?

Communication and Engagement

Chapter 6 provides a guide and resources for potential communication and engagement. This PM Plan section outlines the actual expected activities to keep people informed. What tools does the agency have that can elevate the PM System to keep the information and lessons learned visible to staff? This could include newsletters, standing agenda PM reports/activities at program or department level meetings, bulletin boards, posters, conference presentations and more. Make a plan for consistent communication and commit to it in writing in the plan.

Work Plan

The PM Plan is a comprehensive document outlining the who, what, where, when, how and why related to PM, and if applicable, QI efforts. One pitfall that agencies can experience is creating a document that does a great job restating the mission and vision of the agency and the high-minded hopes for PM, but then is vague about the actual activities taking place throughout the agency to build, support and maintain a culture of PM and QI. A well-defined Work Plan is essential. Once the PM Plan is drafted and finalized, there may be minor changes or adjustments made over time, but the majority of updates will take place within the developed work plan. A PM or PM/QI Work Plan is a summary of activities that will take place over a period of time, preferably in quarterly or bi-annual increments. Prior to developing the work plan, determine if there are other agency initiatives that may need to be considered for alignment. For example, strategic planning. If there is a strategic planning implementation plan that maps out activities for the next two years, stick with that same timeframe to eliminate any possibility of confusion on deadlines with implementation. When the time comes to update strategic planning activities, it will also be time to update PM/QI planning activities.

Meet with the PM/QI Council, or PM support team to review as assessment of the agency with regards to PM. Make sure to have an understanding of current agency activities and structure related to PM/QI, culture, strengths and opportunities for improvement. Brainstorm ideas and activities that could be implemented to move toward a fully integrated PM culture. An example of ideas and activities may include:

- Professional Development Forums for employees to learn about QI, process improvement and hear about best practices
- Evaluate current culture around QI and PM and identify gaps. Develop training around these needs. Training may need to be specific to office/program needs
- Review Quality Culture exercise/assessment results with Senior Leadership Team
- Incorporate introduction to PM/QI into new employee orientation
- Offices/programs to evaluate current performance measures
- Survey employees to determine QI needs, interests and questions
- Develop strategies to address quality and PM gaps
- Educate employees on PM/QI Council
- Council to serve as PM/QI resource for staff to help troubleshoot potential QI issues
- Offices/programs to develop strategies to address PM gaps
- Senior leadership to set and communicate PM/QI priorities to all employees
- Identify additional venues for sharing results and best practices internally and externally
- Work with Senior Leadership to develop a focus on Customers
- Provide training to employees on Customer Satisfaction and the importance of Customer Satisfaction
- Work with all programs to ensure that customer base has been identified (internal and external)
- Provide monthly updates to all staff that highlight PM/QI related efforts
- Design a process for sharing PM data – such as place for shared spreadsheets or a dashboard
- Provide training to employees on PM basics, focused on purpose and measure design
- Identify additional audiences who need to know about PM results, and share reports
- Re-assess Quality Culture and recognize improvements made
- Provide monthly updates to all staff that highlight PM related efforts.
- Adopt criteria for evaluating measures within the regular (monthly/quarterly) PM reports
- Programs to annually review measures for reliability and meaningfulness
- Share PM/QI successes in employee Newsletter

Performance Management Implementation Plan Summary					
	January – May Year 1	June – December Year 1	January – May Year 2	June – December Year 2	Ideas to be Incorporated As Time Permits
Assessment	– Evaluate current culture around QI and PM and identify gaps. Develop training around these needs. Training may need to be specific to office/program needs – Review assessment results with Senior Leadership Team	– Offices/programs to evaluate current performance measures – Offices/programs to develop strategies to address performance management gaps – Re-assess Quality Culture and recognize improvements made	– Survey employees to determine PM/QI needs, interests and questions – Programs to annually review measures for reliability and meaningfulness	– Develop strategies to address quality and performance management gaps – Report progress to Senior Leadership Team	– Revise PM plan to meet the needs moving forward
Communication (Internal & External)	– Senior leadership to set and communicate PM/QI priorities to all employees – Incorporate introduction to PM/QI into the DPH's new employee orientation	– Educate employees on PM/QI Council – Professional development forums for employees to learn about PM and hear about best practices	– Identify additional venues for sharing results and best practices internally and externally – Share PM/QI successes in employee Newsletter	– Communication to all employees regarding results of employee QI survey and QI Council next steps	
Customer Focus	– Work with all programs to ensure that customer base has been identified (internal & external) – Work with Senior Leadership to develop a focus on Customers	– Provide training to employees on Customer Satisfaction and the importance of Customer Satisfaction	– Evaluate Customer Satisfaction data/feedback to identify QI efforts/projects	– Provide training to employees on Customer Satisfaction – Assess utilization of customer satisfaction data to inform program changes/improvements	– Use data regarding percent of staff who have completed Customer Satisfaction Training as an agency-wide performance metric
Performance Management	– Adopt criteria for evaluating measures – Provide monthly updates to all staff that highlight PM/QI related efforts	– Design a process for sharing PM data – Provide training to employees on PM basics	– Council to serve as QI resource for staff to help troubleshoot PM/QII issues	– Provide monthly updates to all staff that highlight PM related efforts	

Figure 7.1 Performance Management Implementation Plan Summary.

Prioritize the list based on effort, impact as well as resources and cost. Determine what can be done within six month time increments, without overwhelming the council, team or employees. Organize the tasks into a summarized table with designated timeframes:

Conclusion

Developing a PM Plan starts with defining what PM is intended to do for the agency. The plan describes the purpose, how PM works, who is involved and the aspirational hopes. The plan can be expected to change from year to year as practice improves the sophistication of the work for all involved. It does not have to start out as a long, comprehensive document. In fact, starting small with a skeleton plan is preferred to delaying progress while all sections are fully designed; just track revisions and updates. Critical components of the plan include a clear focus on activities to support improving and sustaining the PM culture focused through clarity about data collection, monitoring performance and coordinated improvement efforts.

The PM Plan, including the clearly stated written process for implementation is the culmination of all of the components and processes outlined in the previous chapters. The old adage: "Fail to plan; plan to fail" rings true. In systems where results matter and accountability is increasingly in demand, the PM System, supported by a solid plan, is the key.

In conclusion, this book ends as it began. As Dr. Les Beitsch stated in the Foreword:

> Often implementing PM is not easy. Moreover, it is not for the faint of heart or the timid. It is for leaders who genuinely are attracted to leadership roles, who seek to maximize the health impact of the scarce resources the public has entrusted with our agencies.

These practical steps supported by leadership and an engaged staff are a guide for strong hearts and brave practitioners.

References and Resources

1 Moran, J. W. and Duffy, G. L. (n.d.). *Public Health Quality Improvement Encyclopedia.* Retrieved from www.phf.org/resourcestools/Pages/Public_Health_Quality_Improvement_Encyclopedia.aspx

2 Tews, D., Henry, J., Jones, J., VanDerMoere, R. and Madamala, K. (2012, January). *Embracing Quality in Public Health: A Practitioner's Quality Improvement Guidebook.* Retrieved from www.mphiaccredandqi.org/wp-content/uploads/2013/12/2012_02_28_Guidebook_web_v2.pdf

3 Quality Glossary of Terms, Acronyms and Definitions: ASQ. (n.d.). Retrieved December 19, 2019, from https://asq.org/quality-resources/quality-glossary

4 Public Health Accreditation Board. (2013, December). *PHAB Standards and Measures, Version 1.5.* Retrieved 2019, from www.phaboard.org: www.phaboard.org/wp-content/uploads/SM-Version-1.5-Board-adopted-FINAL-01-24-2014.docx.pdf

8 Performance Management Case Studies

NEW MEXICO DEPARTMENT OF HEALTH

Shaza Stevenson and Terry Bryant

Performance management (PM) is a time-tested approach to quality assurance of organizational goals that furthers budgetary accountability. Although different definitions exist, most definitions of PM describe it as the systematic use of organizational performance data within a structured planning framework to inform management decisions and shape program actions for improved organizational effectiveness. Numerous attempts to mandate PM for governmental agencies have been made, and frequently these attempts have been linked to public budgeting. Performance budgeting, and later program budgeting, were important phases in the evolution of public budgeting in the United States, both locally and at the federal level.[1] Over time, these budgetary approaches included an emphasis on what the government does, rather than on what the government purchases, and began to focus on what the government accomplishes, rather than the means of accomplishment. At the same time, and parallel to this evolution, program planning, program evaluation and to a lesser degree PM, were becoming closely associated with each other through the development of program logic models, popularized in the 1990s by the United Way and the Kellogg Foundation.[2]

In 1993, during the "New" Performance Budgeting era,[1] the United States Congress passed the Government Performance and Results Act (GPRA), which was intended to improve governmental PM, gain the trust of the American people and hold the government accountable for program results. The GPRA requires federal agencies to develop strategic plans and long-term results-oriented goals for each of their primary functions. In addition, agencies are required to develop annual performance goals, a plan for meeting goals and a plan for measuring the achievement of goals. Finally, the GPRA requires agencies to report annually on their performance.

Around this time, interest in performance budgeting took hold in state and local governments and led to prioritization of performance measurement in government budgeting processes.[3,4] In 1999, the Accountability in Government Act (AGA) was signed into law in New Mexico. An analysis of the Act indicated that it "would use the state budget process to define outputs, outcomes and performance measures which would be evaluated annually to determine the performance of state government programs and provide more cost-effective and responsive government services."[5] Currently, state agencies in New Mexico are required to develop strategic plans annually, identify performance goals and report on their performance.

Since enactment of the AGA, NMDOH has developed, monitored and reported on numerous performance measures. The NMDOH Performance Management System began to develop around 2011 and matured with the Department's efforts to gain national public health accreditation. The NMDOH was accredited in 2015 by the national Public Health Accreditation Board, and simultaneously moved away from measuring and reporting on program performance strictly as a budgetary or compliance endeavor. Rather than viewing the measurement and reporting of performance as a required activity, the Department developed and adopted a comprehensive PM approach. From the PM perspective, developing, monitoring and reporting on performance became a value-added enterprise that not only enabled the communication of the Department's progress, but began to support progress itself.

Performance Management's Purpose

PM relies on the use of defined outcomes or outputs to cyclically evaluate and respond to performance. To systematically manage organizational performance, an organization regularly measures actual performance results and compares them to planned or intended results. Comparing actual results with intended results provides feedback on the effectiveness of programs and processes. Using this feedback to adjust programs and processes in response to past performance (ideally, through application of quality improvement (QI) strategies) is a definitive hallmark of PM and differentiates PM from performance monitoring or performance reporting.

The Public Health Foundation describes the practices for achieving PM as a Public Health Performance Management Framework. The framework identifies four core practices, supported by five structural components that are necessary to sustain a culture of performance excellence.

A Performance Management System (PM System) is the set of structures, resources and processes dedicated to the consistent and intentional development, implementation, monitoring, evaluation, reporting and improvement of organizational performance. The purpose of a PM System is to foster organizational excellence and ensure accountability. An effective PM System should be:

- Informative to decision makers, partners and stakeholders
- Results-oriented
- Clear and concise
- Valid and reliable
- Economical
- Accessible
- Transparent

In addition, an effective PM System will include measures of the inputs contributed by the organization (e.g., capabilities, resources, activities and programs) and will allow tracking of actions, outputs, outcomes and, ultimately, impact on population health. It will also create organizational alignment and support implementation of strategic priorities.

The NMDOH Strategic Framework

The New Mexico Department of Health (NMDOH) is a centralized system of health services with a Cabinet Secretary, appointed by the Governor, overseeing the Department. New Mexico has 33 counties and 23 American Indian tribes, pueblos and nations with off reservation populations. In accordance with the State Tribal Collaboration Act, all state agencies must collaborate on a government-to-government basis, to promote more effective communication and relationships with the federally recognized tribes, pueblos and nations in New Mexico.

The 33 counties are organized into five public health regions. Governance of these regions is provided by NMDOH and organized to have staff resources in all counties to locally assess and address public health needs. While NMDOH's main campus is located in Santa Fe, there are 56 local public health offices around the state. These local offices provide necessary community-based perspectives, a coordinated service approach and an integral focus on the delivery of public health.

The Department also operates six direct care facilities, oversees three home and community-based Medicaid waiver programs for New Mexicans with developmental disabilities, and serves as the regulatory entity for certain licensed health care facilities.

Combined with the eight divisions that make up NMDOH's organizational structure (Administrative Services, Public Health, Epidemiology and Response, Scientific Laboratory, Developmental Disabilities Support, Health Improvement, Facilities and Medical Cannabis), NMDOH is tasked with wide-ranging duties that formulate a statewide public health system. The

Our Vision	A Healthier New Mexico!					
Our Values	**Accountability**	**Communication**	**Teamwork**	**Respect**	**Leadership**	**Customer Service**
	Honor our commitments with honesty & integrity	Promote trust through mutual, honest and open dialogue	Share expertise and ideas through creative collaboration to work toward common goals	Appreciate the dignity, knowledge and contributions of all persons	Promote growth and lead by example throughout the organization and communities	Place internal and external customers first and assure that their needs are met

Our Goals	**Community Engagement**	**Data & Evaluation**	**Effective Business Practices**	**Employee Competence**	**Healthy New Mexico**
	Improve Organizational Communication & Collaboration	Provide benchmarks for public health practice improvements and monitor NM's health status	Develop policies and plans that support agency-wide health implementation & practice	Assure a competent and sustainable public health workforce	Improve Health Status of all New Mexicans

Our Relationships	**Funders**	**Community Partners**	**Tribes, Pueblos & Nations**	**Policymakers**	**State Agencies**
	• Federal • State • Private: local & national	• Universities & Colleges • Health Councils • Community Centers • Primary Care Organizations & Hospitals • Schools • Nonprofit Organizations • Faith Based Organizations • Corrections & Law Enforcement	• Tribal Communities • Tribal Health Councils • Indian Health Services (IHS) • Bureau of Indian Education & Indian Affairs • Urban Indian Centers • American Indian Educational Institutions	• Governor/Executive Branch • Legislative Branch, including Legislative Finance Committee • Legislative Council Services • Attorney General • Medical & Nursing Boards • Courts	• Department of Finance & Administration • Human Services • Aging and Long-Term Services • Children, Youth & Families • Environment • Transportation • Public Safety & Corrections

Our Mission	Promote Health & Wellness	Improve Health Outcomes	Assure Safety Net Services

Figure 8.1 NMDOH Strategic Framework.

Department pursues its vision and mission through population-based protection and prevention strategies, provision of health statistics and vital records, licensure and certification of health facilities, clinical testing services, access to person-centered community supports, in addition to many other activities.

The Alignment of Key Performance Components

With a push for organizational excellence from public health accreditation, NMDOH institutionalized a system of PM and improvement. This infographic represents the primary system components and how they are linked.

The NMDOH model begins with community health assessments at the local level. These assessments identify key health needs and issues through a comprehensive data collection process. Ideally, community health assessments should directly inform NMDOH's State of Health in New Mexico report, which is an overall state health assessment. The state health assessment evaluates New Mexico's various populations and reflects the big picture of our current state of health in NM.

The statutorily required State Health Improvement Plan (SHIP) is NMDOH's proposed long-term state health plan and uses data from the community and state health assessments to determine the most pressing health priorities. Through the SHIP, evidence-based strategies are developed for

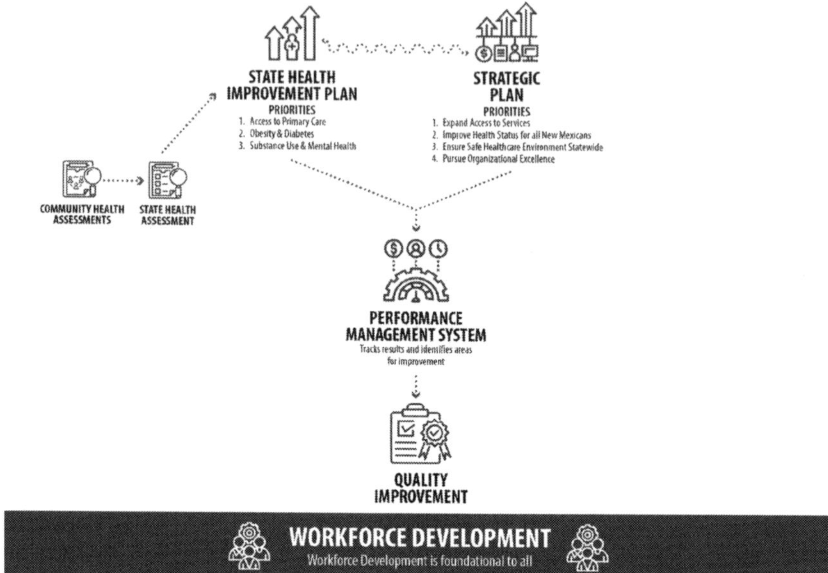

Figure 8.2 Alignment of Key Performance Components.

department action. The SHIP goes beyond DOH's scope and acts as an inter-agency, tribal and community-oriented health improvement plan for the entire state.

The SHIP works in tandem with the strategic plan, but the strategic plan is department specific and guides the department's direction for a three-year period. The strategic plan is fundamental to the department achieving its key objectives and identifying best practices.

NMDOH has established a PM System that goes beyond AGA requirements by determining internal programmatic performance measures as well as statewide population-based indicators and inter-agency strategies via the SHIP. While the AGA measures represent both SHIP and strategic plan priorities, there are areas where it is necessary to monitor and track administrative and operational effectiveness and progress. Ultimately, each division should be strategically aligned with the department's over-all strategic plan by determining suitable internal objectives and corresponding performance measures.

A well-functioning PM System should reveal areas for improvement to NMDOH leadership. When targets are not met, or the expected results fall short, the department's QI system is designed to assist with determining solutions to identified problem areas through targeted QI projects, workforce development and training. NMDOH is committed to continually improving public health workforce competency to support the mission of creating a healthier New Mexico.

Overall, these interrelated components push NMDOH to continuously review and work toward systematic alignment and high performance. With a comprehensive strategic plan, a highly institutionalized PM System, a data driven analysis of New Mexico's health status and the regular determination of state health priorities, NMDOH will continually advance a culture of quality and performance and deliver results to the people of New Mexico.

The NMDOH Performance Management System

To support implementation of the State Health Improvement Plan (SHIP), Strategic Plan, and AGA performance measures and expectations, the PM System is an agency-wide design that has its foundation in a commitment to excellence and a belief that active governance is an effective way to ensure and improve performance, as well as improve health status and outcomes for the state of New Mexico. Further, the PM System conveys an essential linkage between program performance and population health status improvement.

To understand the PM System, it is important to differentiate between measures of health, which NMDOH calls "indicators," and measures of performance on health, which are called "program performance measures" or simply "performance measures." There are three levels of performance accountability and measure setting: population health status, statewide health strategies and program PM. At the population level, a desired condition of well-being for the population is identified and indicators are used to measure population health status. To achieve the desired condition of well-being, the entire health system works collectively to improve health status, as measured by the population-based indicators. The SHIP functions as a statewide health improvement plan and should work in alignment with the collective health system toward the desired population-based indicator's improvement. The success of expansive health status initiatives depends on the SHIP being properly utilized as a document guiding inter-agency responses to identified health priorities. At the NMDOH program level, each member of the department is accountable for their program's performance.

Figure 8.3 demonstrates how the population-based indicator is foundational to SHIP goals and strategies as well as programmatic performance measures. It guides and aligns not only the agency's activities but directs and measures statewide focus toward extensive systemic health shifts that cannot be accomplished alone. When programmatic measures are summed, NMDOH can anticipate seeing them reflected in a change to population health status. In other words, each member of the health system is accountable for their programmatic contribution and the over-all system is accountable for improving population health status.

Substance Use Disorders: Alcohol-Related Death
Population-Based Indicator: Rate of Alcohol Related Deaths in New Mexico
State Health Improvement Plan Goals & Strategies
SHIP Statewide Goal 1: Reduce alcohol-related death – SHIP Strategy 1: Increase the percentage of New Mexicans who have had a Screening & Brief Intervention for alcohol use. – SHIP Strategy 2: Decrease alcohol consumption in counties with the highest alcohol related mortality by creating Behavioral Health Investment Zones for non-Medicaid behavioral health services that will assist the highest priority zones and to develop and implement a plan that addresses the alcohol-related mortality in those counties. – SHIP Strategy 3: Form and maintain a state agency work group to coordinate efforts to reduce alcohol-related mortality. – SHIP Strategy 4: Increase the number of county and tribal health councils that are implementing evidence-based strategies to reduce problem drinking.
AGA & Strategic Plan Performance Measures
Indicator: Rate of alcohol-related deaths per 100,000 population – PM: Percent of persons receiving alcohol screening and brief intervention (a-SBI) services. – PM: Percent of county and tribal health councils that include in their plans evidence-based strategies to reduce alcohol-related harms. – PM: Percent of Medication Assisted Treatment initiations on alcohol and opiate use disorders. – PM: Rate of medical detox occupancy at Turquoise Lodge Hospital. – PM: Percent of priority Request for Treatment clients who are provided admission appointment to Turquoise Lodge's program within 2 days.

Figure 8.3 Substance Use Disorders: Alcohol-Related Death (ERD Performance Measure Example).

In the SHIP, NMDOH identifies the priority population health status indicators it will address, thereby representing the Department's overarching statewide health goals. The strategies outline programmatic efforts that if accomplished, should show progress toward the three-year cycle of the State Health Improvement Plan. For each annual cycle within the three-year Strategic Plan, the Department establishes a set of AGA performance measures that are reported to the legislature and often coincide with the SHIP priorities but can also reflect more broad-ranging departmental activities and legislatively oriented issues.

The Department identifies a performance target for each performance measure. Ideally, a performance measure is established at the beginning of the three-year strategic plan cycle and is used in repeated annual cycles for each of the three years of the strategic plan.

NMDOH Performance Management Operations

The Department's Office of Policy and Accountability (OPA) serves as an administrative hub for the operation of the Department's PM System. OPA provides training and oversight in the development of performance measures and reports on progress. Within each of the Department's eight divisions,

Performance Management Coordinators (PMCs) organize their division's PM work and help integrate and diffuse PM throughout the Department.

All New Mexico state agencies report annually on their AGA measures as part of the budget proposal and PM process. This process also identifies "key" agencies, which are those with large mandates and budgetary responsibility, to report on their performance quarterly and NMDOH is a key agency with quarterly reporting expectations. The annual report summarizes the development of the strategic plan's goals and objectives, and annual progress of the performance measures. This is an opportunity to reassess and review the objectives, activities, measures and targets to account for what has been accomplished, or not, and to look for areas for expansion or improvement.

Currently, the quarterly reports have the performance measure, a results timeline, the target, the measure's description, the data source/methodology, a story behind the data and a quarterly improvement action plan. The "story behind the curve" is contextual information about the measure.

Where progress is not occurring as anticipated, the PM System incorporates the use of QI to accelerate progress. The benefits of the system include:

- Opportunities to build upon existing systems, priorities, agency initiatives and strategic goals.
- Transparency created by setting objectives and establishing metrics for those objectives.
- Improved decision-making for resource allocation.
- Prioritization around a common set of priorities and ways to measure progress.

Senior Leadership reviews all quarterly and annual reports, as well as participates in PM meetings. The Secretary schedules regular quarterly follow-up sessions and in these meetings the progress reports and targets are analyzed, allowing for more contextually nuanced discussions of results not met, the identification of problem areas and the development of improvement plans. The intention is to develop and foster a culture of quality and accountability throughout the department. On a quarterly basis, the Department examines achievements and makes immediate course corrections to maintain the necessary progress.

The NMDOH PM System evidences the core practices, structural components and key attributes of effective PM Systems and is easily recognizable as a framework to support and promote program performance through recurring review and improvement. In a very practical way, achievement or completion of each quarterly report leads to the eventual evaluation of each performance measure's annual target, which in turn should accumulatively show long-term health system changes. Together, providing a quantified assessment on whether the programmatic efforts and improvements positively impact the population's health status as intended.

ERD PERFORMANCE MEASURE #7

Percent of county and tribal health councils that include in their plans evidence-based strategies to reduce alcohol-related harms

Results

FY17	FY18	FY19	FY20 Q1	FY20 Q2	FY20 Q3	FY20 Q4	FY20 Total	FY20 Target
11%	11%	18%	21%	21%				≥ 15%

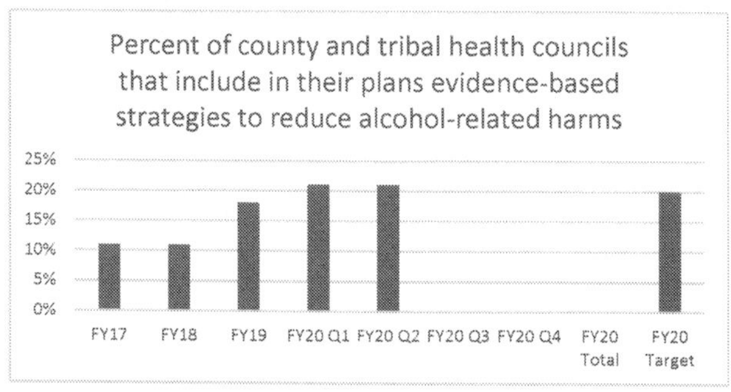

MEASURE DESCRIPTION:
Numerator: Number of health councils that report evidence-based alcohol prevention strategies.
Denominator: Total number of health councils.

DATA SOURCE/METHODOLOGY:
Data for this measure comes from a survey and phone calls.

STORY BEHIND THE DATA:
The county and tribal/national/pueblo health councils, impact health outcomes in their service areas through interventions and programs. Health councils are encouraged to implement evidence-based strategies to prevent excessive alcohol consumption.

IMPROVEMENT ACTION PLAN:

Major Quarterly Action Steps:	Goal Completion Date				
	Q1	Q2	Q3	Q4	Target
1) Contacted Colfax and Eddy County Health Councils	2				2
2) Contacted Grant and Lincoln County Health Councils		2			2

NMDOH reaches out to at least two health councils per quarter to enquire about evidence-based excessive alcohol strategies and offer data and support.

Figure 8.4 Quarterly Report Snapshot.

MONTEREY COUNTY HEALTH DEPARTMENT, CALIFORNIA

Patricia Zerounian, MPP, Management Analyst III, Accreditation and Quality Improvement Manager

> Monterey County Health Department, located on California's central coast, provides 437,000 residents with behavioral health/substance use treatment, clinic services, environmental health protections, emergency medical services, public guardianship and public health services.

Monterey County Health Department (MCHD) launched a pilot program to establish annual performance goals and collect performance measure data in 2011. In ensuing years, MCHD improved and refined its practices for selecting appropriate indicators to represent the department's broad variety of functions; non-burdensome ways to measure the indicators; and how to best communicate results to staff, elected officials and the public. These methods now successfully support more than 50 performance measures for MCHD's seven bureaus, many of which can be longitudinally compared back to 2011.

MCHD's Planning, Evaluation and Policy (PEP) Unit began conducting program evaluation in 2005 for department programs and external organizations that typically included logic modeling, goal and objective setting, indicator identification, and methods to measure performance and progress. These skills proved to be very useful when PEP staff began working with the department's seven bureaus to establish meaningful performance measures.

Selecting Performance Measures

With QI at the forefront, PEP staff determined the importance of tying annual performance measures to *efficiency*, *effectiveness*, *reach*, *equity* and *quality*. PEP further committed to avoiding the "counting widgets" syndrome; greater value was placed on going beyond counting service units and instead examining ways the health department's performance can improve the wellbeing of our county residents. By 2012, MCHD had begun designating its performance measures as being one or a combination of *efficiency*, *effectiveness*, *reach*, *equity* and *quality*.

Over the first few years of measuring performance progress, MCHD learned what worked and what did not, when selecting performance measures. Measuring performance that made sense to the public and reflected community priorities worked; measuring highly technical or short-term performance did not. PEP assembled the lessons learned into a list of five criteria that are applicable to all department functions.

Criteria for Selecting Good Program Measures

1 Performance measures should be easily understood by the public. One of the purposes of performance measurement is to transparently provide the public with progress made in reaching objectives and goals. Performance measures that are overly scientific or obscure are defeating to the purpose of transparency.
2 Performance measures should epitomize the bureau's primary functions. Examples of performance measures that directly relate to public health, for example, may be measuring the timely response to communicable disease outbreaks, the percentage of middle and high schoolers receiving teen pregnancy avoidance education, or the number of mothers who provide any breastfeeding up to 6 months of their child's age. These examples represent the public's expectations of public health education and support services.
3 Performance measures should address the extension of services to people of underserved race/ethnicities, sexual identities, age groups, geographic areas and other variables. Measuring reach into subpopulations helps to maintain focus on providing equitable health services.
4 Performance measures should focus on ongoing activities, and not those that are short-term or grant-funded. Ongoing activity performance measures allow the performance outcomes to be compared over time, with explanations for setbacks (such as staff cutbacks or lack of cross-training), or giant leaps forward. Understanding the history of a program's performance can help avoid pitfalls that might reduce program reach or effectiveness, while understanding the elements that contribute to great gains could help replicate successful methods.
5 Performance measures should reflect the health department's Strategic Plan and Community Health Improvement Plan priorities. MCHD had neither of these plans in 2011, but developed them both as part of the national public health accreditation process. By 2014, MCHD began designating its performance measures as being one or a combination of *efficiency*, *effectiveness*, *reach*, *equity* and *quality*.

Goal Setting

Performance goals should be reachable, and not out of reach or unrealistic. MCHD sometimes sets goals that are similar or identical to the Healthy People goals set by the U.S. Department of Health and Human Services, Office of Disease Prevention and Health Promotion. State and industry goals may also be referenced, but MCHD's more common approach is to look at the department's five to ten-year performance, and set a goal that continues an improvement trend that will eventually reach optimal community health.

This method best reflects the demographic challenges that are unique to each department's service area, and further, accounts for the department's staffing capacities.

For example, MCHD measures the percentage of Women, Infants and Children (WIC) program infants, at ages 6 months and one year old, who are fed exclusively or any breastmilk. The annual targets may be increased based on the actual performance (see Tables 8.1 and 8.2). If the actual performance fluctuates, the QI manager may keep the target steady. If performance improves, the target may be slightly increased. The important aspect of QI it to look for a trend of improvement in the right direction.

Monterey County Breastfeeding Goals for WIC Recipients, FY 2014–15 to FY 2017–18

Table 8.1 Monterey County Health Department Goals for *Exclusive* Breastfeeding

Infant Age		2014–15	2015–16	2016–17	2017–18
6 months (%)	Target	22.0	22.0	22.0	22.0
	Actual	21.6	21.7	21.3	19.9
12 months (%)	Target	18.5	18.5	18.5	19.5
	Actual	19.0	19.5	20.0	18.9

Source: Monterey County Health Department WIC Program.

Note

Exclusive breastfeeding: breastfed infant does not receive any formula from the WIC program.

Table 8.2 Monterey County Health Department Goals for *Any* Breastfeeding

Infant Age		2014–15	2015–16	2016–17	2017–18
6 months (%)	Target	42.5	42.5	42.5	43.5
	Actual	44.3	44.9	46.9	46.0
12 months (%)	Target	36.5	36.5	36.5	37.5
	Actual	41.5	39.2	41.4	39.2

Source: Monterey County Health Department WIC Program.

Note

Any breastfeeding: infant is fed breast milk at least once in a 24-hour period.

Units of Measure

Because populations and workloads are in constant flux, MCHD chooses to measure most of its performance measures in percentages of the whole, for

Monterey County WIC-enrolled Breastfed Infants

Effectiveness Measure Essential Service #2, 3, &7 Strategic Plan Initiative 1, 2, & 3	2016-17 Goal	2017-18 Goal	Q1 Actual	Qt 2 Actual	Qt 3 Actual	Qt 4 Actual	Year to Date Average	% of Annual Goal
Any breastfeeding at 6 months	42.5%	42.5%	44.8%	45.4%	48.5%	45.2%	46.0%	105.7%
Exclusive breastfeeding at 6 months	22.0%	22.0%	19.4%	19.8%	21.9%	18.6%	19.9%	94.9%
Any breastfeeding at 12 months	36.5%	36.5%	41.8%	37.0%	38.6%	39.3%	39.2%	104.5%
Exclusive breastfeeding at 12 months	18.5%	18.5%	20.2%	17.4%	18.2%	19.8%	18.9%	96.9%

What: The any and exclusive breastfeeding rates of infants aged 6 months and one year enrolled in the Women, Infants and Children program. Breastfeeding at 11 months is representative of breastfeeding at one year. Any = infant is fed breast milk at least once in a 24 hour period. Exclusive = breastfed infant does not receive any formula from the WIC program.

Why: Breastfeeding protects infants' and mothers' health and fights diseases such as asthma, diabetes, and obesity.

How are we doing? Monterey County exceeds State average breastfeeding rates.

Figure 8.5 Monterey County Health Department Breastfeeding Goals for WIC recipients, FY 2017–18.

example, percentage of behavioral health clients discharged with treatment goals met or partially met; percentage of clinic services patients aged 21 or older with diabetes who have an HbA1c level at less than 9; or the percentage of hospital birth certificates that are processed within 10 days of birth. Quantities are measured, however, when the denominator is difficult to measure – for example, MCHD measures the pounds of recyclable and other dumped materials collected by volunteers during its annual "County Cleanup" events. The goal for the number of "County Cleanup" volunteers, however, is set as a 10 percent increase over the prior year. Another example of a quantitative measure is the number of high school teens who volunteer to become peer educators in a Youth Leadership Development training program to build self-esteem and resilience.

Performance Measure Tracking and Data Analysis

MCHD tracks annual performance measures on a quarterly basis, using Excel spreadsheets that are posted on SharePoint in a location that is accessible by all Health Department employees. The spreadsheets are maintained by PEP staff, who send quarterly reminders to program staff who are responsible for collecting their performance measure data. The director of Health and bureau chiefs are copied on the reminder emails to help assure that program staff record their data in a timely manner; data recording deadline is within 30 days of the close of each quarter.

The Excel spreadsheets are tabbed by bureau, numbered and designated as (1) *efficiency*, *effectiveness*, *reach*, *equity* or *quality*; (2) the related Essential Service of Public Health; and (3) the related MCHD strategic initiative. The performance measure definition, purpose, goal and quarterly data are recorded, and space titled "How are we doing?" allows program managers to describe reasons for goal achievement or shortfall. Program managers enter the quarterly performance data only, and the spreadsheet is formatted to automatically calculate the Year to Date average and the Percent of Annual Goal achieved, year to date calculation, and percent of annual target achieved. The complete picture of MCHD's priority health performance, how it relates to the purpose of public health and implications for community residents, are thereby represented in table format.

Communicating Performance Outcomes

National Public Health Accreditation requires health departments to inform staff, the public, and government officers and electeds of its performance outcomes (Standard 12.3). In addition to keeping the performance measure tracking spreadsheets in a location that is fully accessible by all staff, MCHD also creates 24" by 36" wall posters showing mid-year and year-end performance

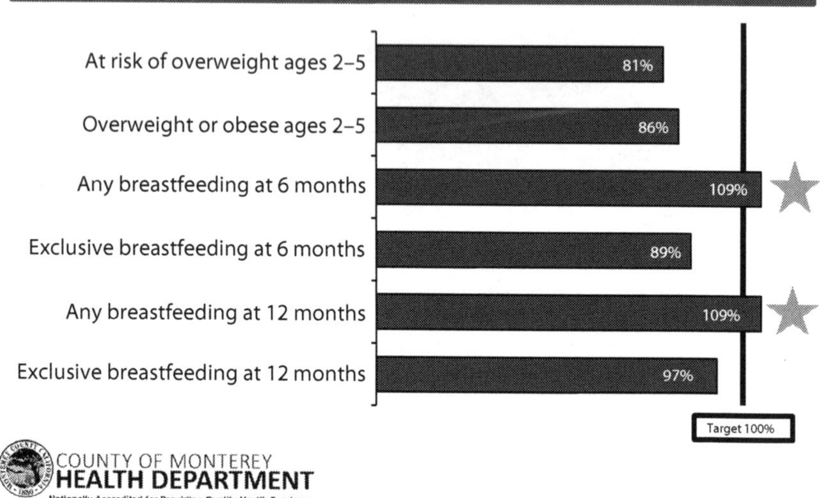

Figure 8.6 Public Health – WIC Performance Measures.

for bureaus to post on walls where they can be seen by staff and the public. To avoid being overly-complicated, the posters only illustrate the performance as it relates to the annual goal. The posters are also replicated and celebrated in MCHD's weekly staff newsletter. The Department devotes a webpage to the practices of PM, with links to current bureau performance measures and outcomes (www.co.monterey.ca.us/government/departments-a-h/health/general/performance-management). The department provides the county board of supervisors with an annual presentation of performance outcomes, and many of MCHD's performance measures are featured in the county's annual recommended budget book.

Quality Improvement

From 2014 through 2016, more than 130 of MCHD's staff in seven cohorts were trained in the Plan, Do, Study, Act (PDSA) method of QI by Public Health Foundation instructors. The one and one-half day training included hands-on learning in small teams, using a wide variety of planning and analysis tools. Each team was engaged in a QI project by the end of their cohort training session. Teams comprised of a single-bureau generally focused on bureau-specific projects, while teams consisting of members from more than one bureau worked at the department level to address issues that affected nearly all staff. All projects were identified as focused on *efficiency*, *effectiveness*, *reach*, *equity*, *quality* or a combination thereof. All QI methods, forms and completed projects are accessible to all staff on in the department's SharePoint QI library. Posters illustrating QI Success Stories are framed and hung in the department's Administration Building lobby, and have been presented at nationwide conferences. All staff who have completed the QI training are presented with a QI chrome emblem to wear on their Department ID badge.

Examples of Completed Monterey County Health Department QI Projects

Celebration

QI projects are hard work requiring thinking innovatively, exploring possibilities, negotiating with colleagues and occasionally going back to the drawing board. MCHD recognizes the work of QI teams by celebrating the accomplishments at the time the Quality Oversight Committee (described below) accepts the project results and approves a new policy or procedure. Our celebrations

Figure 8.7 Success Story LGBTQ QI Project.

Figure 8.8 Success Story WikiHiki QI Project.

include a personal congratulations from our department Director and the staff Bureau Chiefs, a framed QI certificate to display at the staff worksite and a number of celebratory trinkets (including chocolate!) that can be purchased at a dollar store. Recognition is given to the QI team members with a full description of the project in the department's newsletter that is distributed to all staff.

Performance Measurement

Performance measurement is one element in MCHD's Quality Management Initiative (QMI) that meets National Public Health Accreditation Standards 9.1 and 9.2. Specifically, MCHD quantitatively measures its progress to achieve our health objectives (Standard 9.1), and uses the progress data to develop and implement QI processes. The integration of performance data and QI activities informs a health department's practices, programs and interventions (Standard 9.2). For clarity, MCHD included these definitions in its formally adopted Quality Management Policy:

> *Performance management* (PM) is the systematic collection of performance data and comparing those data to intended goals, thereby tracking progress and identifying opportunities for even greater improvements.

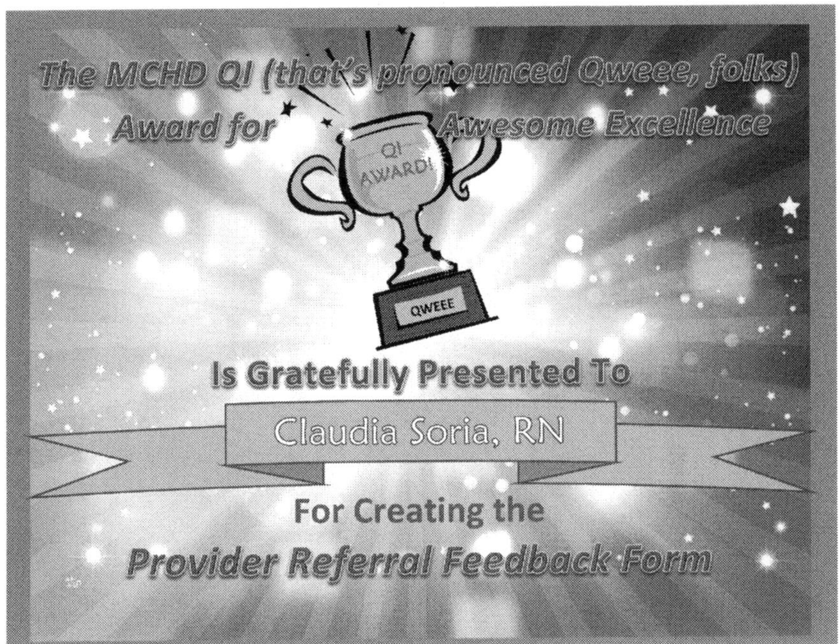

Figure 8.9 QI Award for Awesome Excellence.

> *Quality improvement* (QI) is a deliberate, iterative process focused on activities that respond to community-identified needs for improving population health through program and organizational *efficiency*, *effectiveness*, *reach*, *equity*, or *quality*.

MCHD merged PM and QI functions into one Quality Management Initiative (QMI) that was adopted as a department policy. The effort is headed by the Quality Oversight Committee (see A. in Figure 8.10), which is a subgroup of the department's Executive Management Team. Proposals can be brought before the Quality Oversight Committee in two ways: through the Performance Management and Innovations Team (PMIT) that is responsible for Strategic Plan updates and other "Big Picture" policy innovations, or through the Public Health Foundation trained-QI Team Leaders and Members. Proposals require approvals before major work on proposed improvements commence. The Quality Oversight Committee may also assign QI projects to the Policy Response and Review Team.

Monterey County Health Department Quality Management Initiative: Operating Structure

To explain further, the Performance Management and Innovation Team (see box B. in Figure 8.10) meets regularly to engage in these functions:

- Strategic Plan: sets the agenda for implementation and periodic updates.
- Community Health Improvement Plan (CHIP): reviews CHIP recommendations.
- Innovation: provides staff with a forum to propose policies, system changes or other innovations that will further MCHD goals.
- Quality Improvement Plan and Workforce Development Plan: Provides input to the plans as a tool for creating a learning organization and maintaining a supportive work environment.

The QI Team Leaders and Members QI Teams (see box C. in Figure 8.10) consist of staff at all levels who have been formally or informally trained in QI tools and techniques. Teams form among staff who volunteer to work on ad hoc QI projects that will improve *efficiency*, *effectiveness*, *reach*, *equity* or *quality*. Upon completion of the QI project, the results and recommendations are submitted to the QI Council for approval or revision, as outlined in Figure 8.10. Each QI team has a Team Facilitator who is responsible for ushering the QI Team process and a Team Sponsor who assists with cross-bureau coordination as needed.

The Policy Response and Review Team (see D. in Figure 8.10) has two functions. First, it responds to Quality Oversight Committee assignments to develop new policies as needs arise. This team works solely with the Committee until the newly created policy is approved for submittal to the MCHD Executive Team. Any needed revisions are referred back to the Second, it monitors the review schedule for existing policies to assure they are periodically reviewed and updated as needed.

Lessons Learned

Our most valuable experience has been the beneficial skills gained by staff who attended formal QI training and who have continued to weave QI into their daily tasks. Small improvements can sometimes create great impacts on the services we offer to our residents. For that reason, we remain dedicated to QI staff training and publicizing completed QI projects to all staff and our Board of Supervisors. Our Performance Management and Quality Improvement Plan was deemed to be "fully demonstrated" in response to national Public Health Accreditation requirements, and the California Department of Healthcare Services has approved of all 27 QI projects submitted thus far to

Figure 8.10 Monterey County Health Department Quality Management Initiative Operating Structure.

benefit our Whole Person Care program to provide comprehensive, coordinated case management for our county's unsheltered populations.

Monterey County's Board of Supervisors and County Administrative Office consider MCHD's PM and QI strategies to be successful examples for other county departments. Most of the completed QI projects achieve efficiencies in staff time which, in turn, free up staff to turn their attention to greater reach into the populations of focus. Not surprisingly, staff's most commonly expressed challenge is identifying time in their workloads to devote to introspective examination. Staff have shown themselves to be more likely to explore QI ideas within their regular teams even while cross-team and cross-bureau QI projects were said to be especially rewarding.

In response to time challenges, the Department's QI manager created and conducted a half-day "Rapid Quality Improvement Solution Symposium" in 2017 to train new employees and refresh the enthusiasm of those previously trained. The agenda included QI project presentations by teams; a discussion of quick wins, little victories and elephants in the room; a presentation of rapid QI methods; two group exercises ("How do you process?" "How do you measure?"); and a decision guide for selecting rapid QI projects. The training session attended by 47 staff members wrapped up with Dr. Phillip Kim's TED Talk, "Chase One Rabbit: The Power of Small Wins" (www.youtube.com/watch?v=oOrX-M-dkSI).

Our next step is to take our "Solution Symposium" on the road: many of our 35 locations are located far from each other. Trainings conducted in team workplaces can boost enthusiasm for QI and avoid the "business as usual" or worse, crisis management styles that can become entrenched if QI thinking and methods become rusty.

SPRINGFIELD-GREENE COUNTY HEALTH DEPARTMENT, MISSOURI

Jordan Coiner, Andee Elmore, Danielle Dingman

Background

Located in southwest Missouri, Springfield is the third largest city in the state behind Kansas City and St. Louis and is home to Springfield-Greene County Health Department (SGCHD). SGCHD is a city-county health department governed by its city council/county commission and serves a population of approximately 290,000 citizens with a staff of about 110 members. The core work of public health is focused on reducing the leading causes of preventable death, with a special focus on underserved populations and health disparities. SGCHD supports this focus through its vision of "Helping People Live Longer, Healthier, Happier Lives."

Several years ago, SGCHD began the process of national accreditation through the Public Health Accreditation Board (PHAB). Some of the requirements of PHAB include:

Community Health Assessment – intended to explore and assess the unique health needs of the community.

Community Health Improvement Plan – describes how the Health Department and local health systems will collaborate to address the unique health needs of the community.

Departmental Strategic Plan – outlines the activities and areas of focus for SGCHD over a 3–5-year period.

Additionally, through the accreditation process, SGCHD recognized the importance of PM oversight, a system for QI, workforce development and the value of data-driven decision making. Previously, all components were present and operational, but disjointed within the department. There was no system in place to ensure these pieces were working together to support, inform and direct the work across the department. Programs were siloed, staff was disengaged and communication suffered as a result.

Recognizing the need for a cultural shift department-wide, the SGCHD began the implementation of "Public Health 3.0." Public Health 3.0 emphasizes cross-sectoral collaboration and the use of timely and locally relevant data and analytics to support comprehensive public health protection. Public Health 3.0 urges public health departments to develop new skill sets, break down funding silos and evolve into the Chief Health Strategists in their communities. To do this, data-driven decision making must inform and align community resources to improve specific health outcomes. More importantly, the Department must make it a priority to work with all relevant community partners to drive initiatives explicitly addressing upstream public health issues.

The first step to encourage a cultural shift was the development of a Quality Council. The "Improvement Teams" paper by the U.S. Department of Health and Human Services Health Resources and Services Administration (HRSA) states "growth as a team evolves into a cohesive entity with a single focus." Establishment of the Quality Council brings together a PM team and a QI team under a Quality Council Board. Initially, SGCHD developed a quality council to "check a box," but through the accreditation process, realized the importance a quality council has in the department and community. The Quality Council Board worked together to build the concept of the Organizational Performance Management System (OPMS), striving for that "single focus."

Organizational Performance Management System

In its infancy, the OPMS was conceptualized by a team of creative whiteboard thinkers within the Department, who formed a framework to visually present the key constructs of the system. The framework is not designed to be an absolute solution to solve organizational questions. Rather, it is a tool to guide efforts and provide a blueprint for how the Department will work to reach programmatic and organizational goals. Additionally, it is designed to foster inclusion and communication between all levels of the Department.

There are six key features of the OPMS framework:

- Organizational PM cycle
- Bi-directional feedback
- Alignment of strategic and operational planning
- Health equity considerations
- Data-driven decision making
- Program-based PM and QI

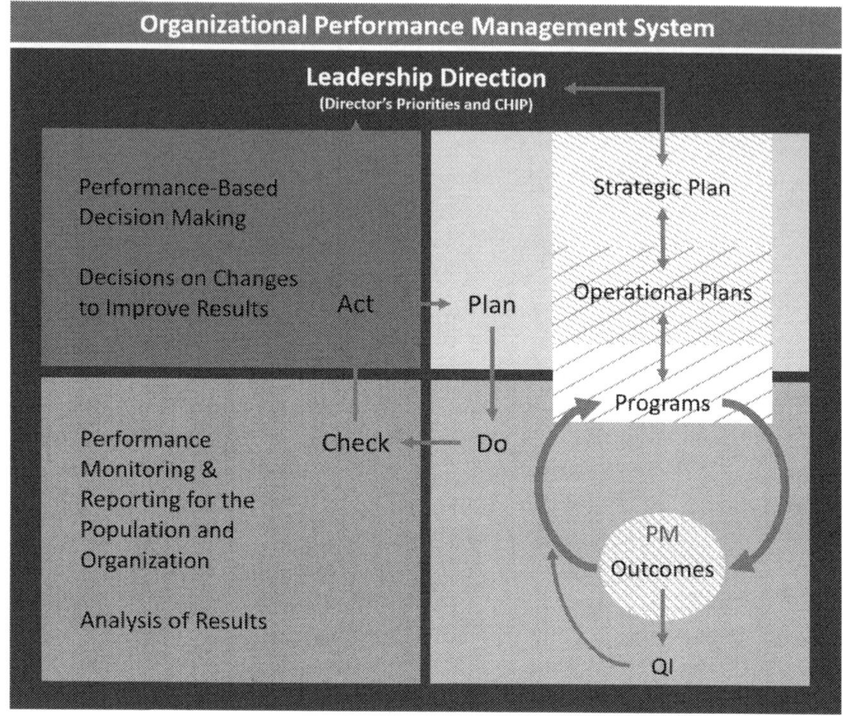

Figure 8.11 Organizational Performance Management System.

The framework is structured around a traditional Plan-Do-Check-Act (PDCA) cycle with each phase of the cycle representing a quadrant that hosts organizational and program planning, program implementation, monitoring and data-driven decision making. The cycle begins with direction provided by Department directors and the Community Health Improvement Plan (CHIP).

"Plan" Phase

The "Plan" phase includes the development of the Strategic Plan and Operational Plan. Bi-directional feedback between program staff and the director's office is a key component of the framework as it encourages involvement and support from all levels of staff. In the "Plan" phase, the development of the Operational Plan includes the Quality Facilitation Team, a subset of SGCHD Quality Council, working directly with program managers and key staff to develop logic models and program plans for each program area. A logic model is a tool used to evaluate the effectiveness of a program. A program plan is intended to outline the activities that staff will follow to reach the goals of the program. These individual meetings produce a set of themes that influence department-wide strategic goals and objectives that are incorporated into the Strategic Plan.

Strategic Plan

To underscore the importance of strategic plan incorporation and alignment within the OPMS framework, it is important to address past lessons learned. The initial Strategic Plan was developed by a committee that represented approximately 10 percent of staff across all program areas of the Department. The Plan met the requirement for PHAB and was established as a 5-year Plan. As program staff attempted to incorporate strategies and activities from the previous Plan into daily work, the Department stumbled through the process. Key staff had little input and did not fully understand the implementation and progress measurement on planned activities. This became a barrier to meeting goals and objectives. The Strategic Plan was not effective, and staff were not fully engaged. Staff were essentially spectators of the Plan because they had not been included in the development.

One major change SGCHD made in the process for strategic planning moving forward was to separate the document into a department Strategic Plan and a division Operational Plan. Strategic priorities are now developed based on:

- Director's vision for the future of public health in Greene County
- Thematic issues resulting from a series of employee listening sessions conducted by the Director
- Cross-cutting themes resulting from the development of program area logic models

It was especially important that these department-wide areas be addressed at the Department leadership level to ensure decision makers within the department have the opportunity to directly affect change. The intent of the Strategic Plan is to set the foundation for work over the next 3–5 years. Goals and objectives are tasked to those in leadership positions.

The priority areas over the course of the Strategic Plan will focus on:

- Community health
- Sustainability
- Innovation
- Workforce development
- Communication

Several cross-cutting themes emerged from logic model development. A need for:

- The development of a feedback loop for referral processes
- Improved internal and external communications
- Enhanced workforce development
- New strategies for funding

An Implementation Plan was created to ensure sufficient progress toward achieving these goals and objectives occurs over the coming years.

Operational Plan

The partner to the Strategic Plan is the Operational Plan. The Operational Plan is a compilation of program plan activities intended to meet the outcomes identified through the development of program area logic models. Each program area has a unique program plan that is created by its near-sighted visionaries – at the grassroots level. Staff that address the needs of the community on a daily basis work together to establish the set of measurable activities to reach the outcomes. Failure to seek input from staff members who work daily with our community results in missed opportunities to reach outcomes and achieve the mission of the department.

A health equity lens is applied in the development of the Strategic and Operational Plans. This considers how program efforts affect specific populations and how efforts should be tailored to address specific community health issues facing the population. Additionally, the Operational Plan (logic models and program plans) is built on the foundation of data-driven decision-making. This approach encourages programs to identify specific desired outcomes and establish measurable strategies and activities to achieve those outcomes. Data-driven decision making is supported by PM to ensure program staff has the tools needed to easily track and evaluate progress.

Program Plans: Logic Models

Through research and discussion, the Quality Council decided to use a model similar to the Grantsmanship Center's 4-square logic model. The purpose of the logic model is to assess and evaluate the program and to ensure mission alignment. This process resulted in an "elevator speech" for each program area and provided staff a platform from which to explain the critical components of the program.

The first square of the logic model contains the problem the program aims to address. The second square contains the perceived causes of the problem. The third square contains the methods the program plans to carry out to

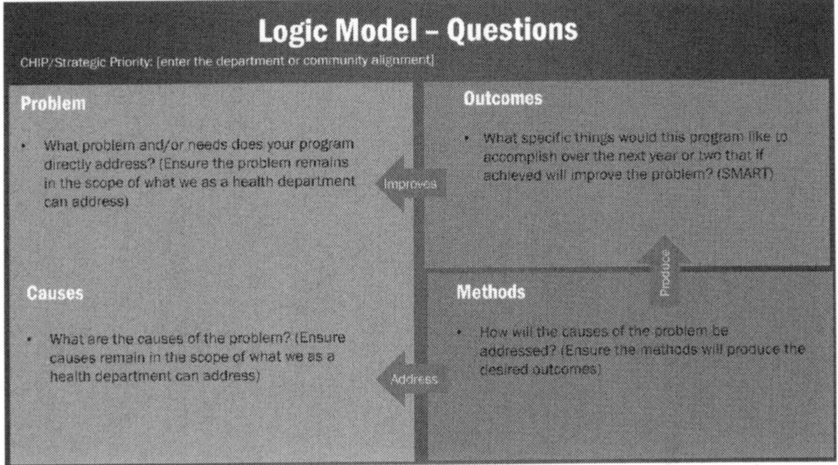

Figure 8.12 Logic Model Questions.

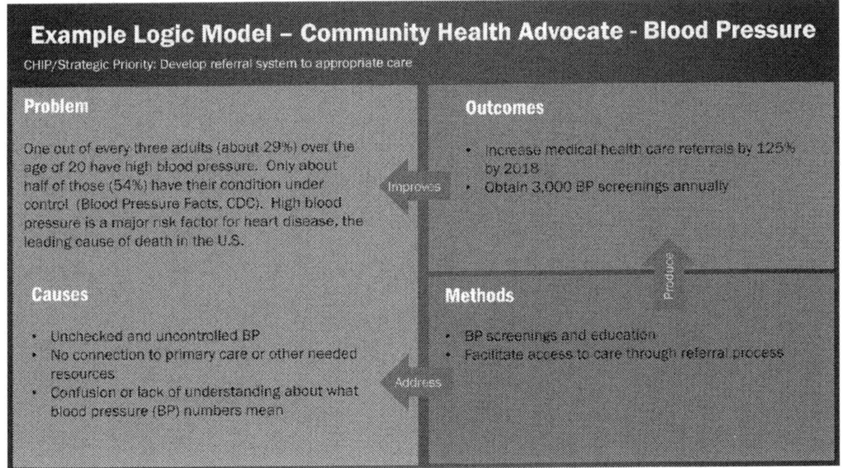

Figure 8.13 Example Logic Model – Community Health Advocate – Blood Pressure.

impact the causes of the problem. Last, the fourth square holds the outcomes the program anticipates achieving in the near future. Logic models were created for both department-wide priorities initiated by the Director's Office, as well as at the program level. The following questions were used to aid in the discussion for each logic model session:

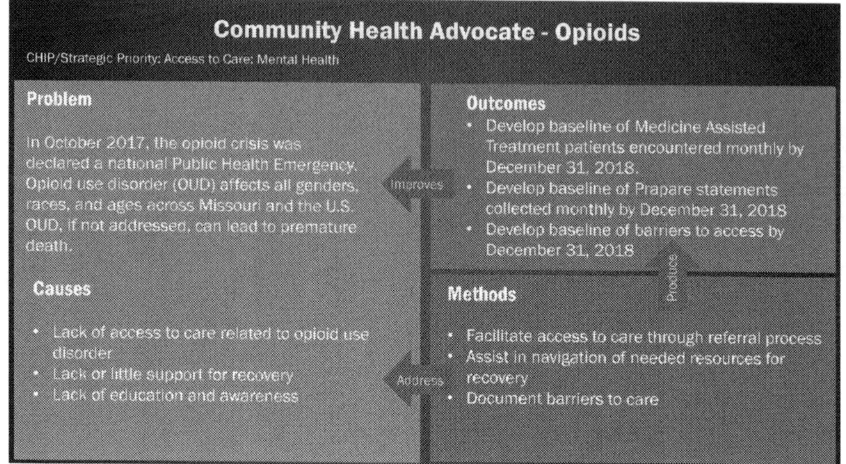

Figure 8.14 Example Logic Model – Community Health Advocate – Opioids.

If one program addresses different problems, separate logic models are needed to outline the different causes, methods and outcomes associated with the problem. The Community Health Advocate example shown below outlines the two program areas that make up the program:

Program Plans: Workbooks

For each program, workbooks are created to provide an organized method for data and information compilation. Five components make up each program area's workbook:

- logic model
- program plan
- data management
- strength, weakness, opportunities and threats (SWOT) analysis
- health equity considerations

Additionally, the program plan tab within the workbook outlines three categories of information: outcomes, strategies and activities. Each outcome identified in the program plan has strategies and activities decided upon and assigned to staff. Assurance of completion of activities by staff is accomplished through accountability check-ins as well as annual performance evaluations. By tasking staff with a set of activities for which input is considered, buy-in and empowerment are natural by-products.

"Do" Phase

Program plans are implemented in the "Do" phase of the OPMS framework. The plans facilitate the day-to-day operations of programs to produce a set of outcomes. Those outcomes are monitored through quarterly PM check-ins. Key metrics are developed and evaluated to determine if QI is to be initiated. Programs engage in continuous PDCA cycles to ensure program work is effectively and efficiently meeting program objectives.

Performance Management and Quality Improvement

The inclusion of both PM and QI to the PDCA cycle ensures another set of resources are available to staff carrying out the strategies and activities of program plans. The first step in building a foundation of PM and QI is to instill basic QI principles into program assessment. Quarterly meetings are the ideal place to include feedback to the Performance Management Committee as to progress being made, as well as the struggles encountered by staff in completing work. If needed, PM and QI work together to initiate a QI project to address problems encountered in achieving outcomes.

"Check" Phase

The sum of the work at the program level is evaluated within the "Check" phase of the organizational PDCA cycle. Evaluation will occur during quarterly check-ins by program leadership and staff. Additional support will be provided by the PM and QI teams to ensure the Department is meeting the goals and objectives outlined in the Strategic and Operational Plans.

"Act" Phase

Department-wide performance, community needs and multi-sectoral partnerships determine actions taken within the "Act" phase. At this phase, Department Leadership determines whether adjustments or corrective actions are needed at the department level to ensure alignment with our Mission.

Flexibility and Accountability

Two key competencies of the OPMS that are not explicitly stated above are flexibility and accountability. Programs and teams have varying needs, different dynamics and unique ways of achieving program goals. Although the framework appears static and potentially unyielding, it is imperative that those leading the implementation of the OPMS acknowledge nuances of programs and work alongside staff to help develop, monitor and respond to performance measures while ensuring the department is collectively moving toward organizational goals. Flexibility does not mean programs are no longer accountable for the work. Rather, it fosters accountability by allowing program staff to take ownership within the context of department-wide progress. Leaders of the OPMS are responsible for educating staff on how the work helps move the Department forward and equipping them with the tools needed to achieve their programmatic goals.

Roles and Responsibilities

Upon acceptance of the OPMS by Department Leadership, the process of educating staff begins. One of the most important aspects of the OPMS is the connection and communication between staff from the bottom to the top and vice versa. The OPMS has been the catalyst to spark a department-wide culture shift and set SGCHD on track to become a high-achieving health department. It is important that communication remains constant from both the top-down and bottom-up in order to foster a true change in culture.

Quality Council

At SGHCD, a Quality Council facilitates the OPMS with guidance from the HRSA document. Quality Council and Committee members were selected through a department-wide application process. Members were selected based on the ability to be flexible, embrace diverse ideas, constructively address conflict and work toward achieving team goals. The Quality Council includes representation from each division of the department, as well as active participation from department leadership.

The Quality Council is led by the Council Chair and Facilitator. Together, the Chair and Facilitator plan for bi-monthly council meetings through reviewing meeting minutes, preparing meeting agendas and distributing pertinent meeting information to council members. The Chair leads meetings, while the Facilitator ensures conversations are meaningful in achieving the objectives of the meeting.

The Facilitator also works on the three-person action-oriented Quality Facilitation Team, a subset of the Quality Council that manages the implementation of the OPMS. This team includes the Facilitator of the Quality Council and the leaders of the Performance Management and Quality Improvement Committees. Staff members within each program area interact one on one with the Quality Facilitation Team to develop a series of logic models, program plans and a system for outcome monitoring.

Performance Management and Quality Improvement

PM and QI committees are composed of five to six individuals with representation from each division in the department. The members are mostly front-line program staff who are responsible for promoting, encouraging and facilitating the monitoring of program performance goals. This group may also identify potential QI projects. The Quality Facilitation Team provides the tools these members need to be champions of PM and QI within their respective divisions. There is equal representation of each division across both committees so that each PM committee member is teamed with a QI committee member to partner in achieving PM and QI goals.

Moving forward, PM and QI committees will mesh with daily activities throughout the department. Committee members will be assigned to teams within the division they normal work. It will be up to the teams to evaluate the status of programs and bring issues that arise back to the PM and QI council for further assessment. Attempts to support and provide solutions will be carried out by the PM and QI members and any additional support needed will be provided by the council. Though these may seem like small steps, they will be huge in building and maintaining a culture of QI in the department.

PM and QI members will work as a team within their respective divisions to break down the outcomes set in each program area's logic model into measurable goals that will be monitored on a quarterly basis. For programs struggling to meet the goals, communication and documentation are important in determining what is working and what is not working. Bi-directional communication from the frontline staff up to the managers and PM and QI teams will ensure support is provided where it is needed.

To empower the workforce and provide support and solutions, it is vital that the PM and QI teams become integrated within the department and are welcomed into program conversations. The role of the PM and QI teams will be to ask strategic questions during program conversations. The questions will ensure that conversations produce actionable next steps to improve the management of the program, the quality of work being done, or both.

If PM and QI teams are able to maintain this role within the department and consistently ask these questions we believe that a culture change will continue to occur. Our hope is that we will begin to see QI projects initiated from the front-line staff in a hope to improve the way they do their jobs and ultimately improve our health department.

Program Managers

Program managers will meet with staff individually on a quarterly basis to determine the progress toward outcomes to which they have been assigned, what has worked and what has not worked, and what needs to be accomplished over the next quarter to continue striving toward meeting those goals. Though the meetings will only be happening quarterly, it is important to note that data collection and maintenance will happen on an ongoing basis in most programs to ensure constant conversation around the outcomes of the program.

On-Line Platform

To allow for interaction and clear understanding of the Strategic, Operational and Workforce development plans, the department is using a web-based story-telling platform. Through this platform, clean templates can be created that outline the goals our department aims to achieve in our Strategic Plan and the goals each individual program area is working toward in the Operational Plans. Best of all, they will all be in one location and easy to access for all staff.

Lessons Learned

Many lessons were learned throughout this process. They included:

- Leadership buy-in is crucial
- The OPMS is a large and complex project that requires time and resources
- The OPMS aims to break down silos
- The OPMS moves staff from spectators to participants
- Every program is unique

Leadership Buy-in

From the beginning, Leadership has been involved and supported the project. Without this support, there would not have been near enough momentum to be where we are at this point in time.

Large Project

This project took a lot of time and effort from several different staff. In addition, meetings with each individual program area had to take place in order to have conversations to create logic models. Without this effort and involvement from staff, the logic models and program plans would not have been completed.

Breaks Down Silos

Communication has been a focal point of this project. With communication at the forefront of minds in every aspect of the project, it has improved drastically and in turn has been successful in breaking down silos throughout the department.

Spectators to Participants

To ensure a culture change in the department, it was vital to jump start staff participation. Allowing staff the opportunity for involvement throughout the process led to a high participation rate and more buy-in of the new system as a whole.

Programs are Unique

The process was not a one-size-fits-all approach and each program area is unique. This resulted in each program area needing its own conversation. Additionally, some programs were more mature than others in some respects. This meant that each program had to be met where they were, and the process had to be tailored to the program's unique needs to ensure success.

Summary

Through the acceptance, implementation and ongoing efforts of the OPMS, SGCHD is now in the early phases of witnessing culture shift across the department. The concepts are beginning to take hold, and there is good support from leadership, administration and program managers. The most important growth and most impactful change is expected at the grass-roots level. Success of this design will be measured by consistency in quarterly meetings with feedback obtained from front-line staff. Additionally, it is expected that staff will vocalize ideas for QI projects and will result in continuous QI across SGCHD.

What began as an effort to earn accreditation status evolved into a mission to transform the department from the inside-out. Over time, the OPMS will become ingrained in the culture of the department and the framework will foster a sustainable approach to align PM, QI, workforce development and data-driven decision making. The OPMS will allow the department to become more effective and efficient in "helping people live longer, healthier, happier lives."

References and Resources

1 Tyer, C. and Willand, J. (1997). Public Budgeting in America: A Twentieth Century Retrospective. *Journal of Public Budgeting, Accounting, and Financial Management*, 9(2), 189–219, https://doi.org/10.1108/JPBAFM-09-02-1997-B001

2 Williams, D. (2014). The Evolution of the Performance Management Model from Black Box to the Logic Model Through Systems Thinking. *International Journal of Public Administration*, 37(13), 932–944. doi: 10.1080/01900692.2014.944989

3 National Governors' Association Task Force on State Management. Gerry Feinstein, Editor (1993). An Action Agenda to Redesign State Government: Reports of the State Management Task Force Strategy Groups. Washington, DC: National Governors Association.

4 Theodore H. Poister and Gregory Streib (1999). Performance Measurement in Municipal Government: Assessing the State of the Practice. *Public Administration Review*, 59(4), 325–335.

5 Patel (1999). House Bill 37 Fiscal Impact Report. Retrieved from New Mexico Legislative Council Services Archives, August 30, 2018.

Appendix

Aligning Accreditation Plans:
A Crosswalk of Plan Requirements in the Public Health Accreditation Boar Standards and Measures, V 1.5

Sonja Armbruster, MA and Margie Beaudry, MA

December 2015

The Public Health Accreditation Board (PHAB) requires health departments to acknowledge that the following plans/policies/systems are substantially developed and near completion prior to applying for voluntary public health accreditation[1]:

- State/Community Health Assessment (S/CHA)
- Organizational Branding Strategy (OBS)
- State/Community Health Improvement Plan (S/CHIP)
- Agency Strategic Plan (SP)
- Workforce Development Plan (WDP)
- Performance Management Policy/System (PMS)
- Quality Improvement Plan (QIP)
- Public Health Emergency Operations Plan[2]

PHAB's goal of "transforming agencies" is best served when these documents[1] are mutually reinforcin so that they together comprise a well-integrated, systematic approach. It may not be feasible for a health department to develop all of these plans simultaneously; however, when a health department writes some plans before others, it risks missing opportunities for alignment that will strengthen all plans. This crosswalk can be part of a conscious effort to coordinate the elements of plans that may n(be created at the same time.

The first wave of accredited health departments primarily focused the early part of their accreditation journeys on the three PHAB "prerequisites": the S/CHA, S/CHIP, and SP. Once these neared completion, accreditation teams turned their attention to the additional, inter-related requirements including several more plan, policy, and system documents. The 2015 updates to PHAB's *Guide to Public Health Accreditation* reinforce the value of developing these documents in a coordinated fashio

Tips for Interpreting the Crosswalk Table

The orientation of the table is to read the rows horizontally. In the first row of the Crosswalk, the S/CHA is noted in the shaded box as being defined in PHAB standard 1.1 with specific reference to the S/CHIP. Wherever text is italicized, we are suggesting a possible connection that is not directly stated in the description requirements in listed in the shaded box. For example, PHAB standard 1.1 does not specifically mention the performance management system, but 1.1 does reference a need for convening partners and ongoing data analysis; these are italicized because while not required, they might be monitored through the PMS.

Like most important efforts, the process, the work, and the outcomes are what's critical, not the report: That said, the reports are the necessary documentation for accreditation and for increased accountability within agencies and with community partners. It is helpful to have a deep understanding of what is required to assure that the work is comprehensive and will not require re-work.

---

[1] http://www.phaboard.org/wp-content/uploads/summary-table-of-revisions-081715.pdf

[2] The Public Health Emergency Operations Plan does not appear in this crosswalk because it can be developed independently; there are no stated or implied links to the other plan documents.

Figure A.1 PHAB Alignment Accreditation Plans Crosswalk. *continued*

Aligning Plans

A Crosswalk of Plan Requirements in the Public Health Accreditation Board Standards and Measures, V 1.5

	S/CHA	OBS	S/CHIP	SP	WDP	PMS	QIP
S/CHA	1.1		1.1.2 Significance: The health assessment provides the basis for the development of the health improvement plan.			*(1.1.1 Regular meetings of health collaborations 1.1.2 The ongoing monitoring, refreshing, and adding of data and data analysis)*	
OBS		3.2.2		3.2.2.1 f. link the branding strategy to the department's strategic plan			
S/CHIP	5.2 The CHIP is a long-term systematic plan to address issues identified in the…CHA.		5.2	(5.2 Conduct a comprehensive planning process resulting in a CHIP)		*(4.1.1.1 Collaborative partnerships; 5.2.2 …individual(s) … that have accepted responsibility for implementing strategies …in the CHIP)*	
SP		5.3.2 d. SP… must consider capacity for and enhancement of … communication (including branding)	5.3.2 g: linkages with the health improvement plan where appropriate	5.3	5.3.2 d: SP must consider …workforce development	5.3.2 c: goals and objectives with measureable time-framed targets	5.3.2g: linkages with the quality improvement plan where appropriate
WDP				Domain 8: "A strategic workforce includes the alignment of workforce development with the	8.2.1	*(8.2.3 …to assess the health department's comprehensive approach to the*	

Figure A.1 Continued

Aligning Plans

A Crosswalk of Plan Requirements in the Public Health Accreditation Board Standards and Measures, V 1.5

PHF

	S/CHA	OBS	S/CHIP	SP	WDP	PMS	QIP
				health department's overall mission and goals and development of strategies for acquiring, developing and retaining staff." (189)		*provision of opportunities for professional career development… and staff development.)*	
PMS				9.1.1.1: leadership's engagement with establishing PMS… documentation could include strategic plans.	9.1.1.1 leadership's engagement with establishing PMS… documentation could include … training programs. 9.1.5.1: Staff development in performance management	9.1	9.1.3.4 Analysis of progress toward achieving goals and objectives and identification of areas in need of focused improvement processes
QIP			9.2.1 Significance: This plan is guided by the health department's… health improvement plan.	9.2.1 Significance: This plan is guided by the health department's… strategic plan. Guidance: The plan must address: Describe and demonstrate how improvement projects align with the health department's strategic vision/mission.	9.2.1 QI Plan Requirements: Quality improvement training, examples: new employee orientation; introductory course for all staff; advanced training for lead QI staff; continuing staff training on QI	9.2.1 QI Plan Requirements: Process to assess the effectiveness of the quality improvement plan and activities	9.2

Figure A.1 Continued

GOALS/OBJECTIVES/MEASURES WORKSHEET

STEP 1
What are two goals that your agency, office or program would like to accomplish to impact health outcomes, or the level of customer service that you provide?

	GOAL #1	GOAL #2
STEP 1	Type agency/division Goal #1 here	Type agency/division Goal #2 here

STEP 2
What are two to three objectives that you would like/need to accomplish to help you meet your overall goals?

STEP 3
What are two to three measures that can be used to demonstrate whether or not you are meeting your desired objective? Something that can be measured monthly, quarterly, or bi-annually.

Objective #1 | Objective #1

Measures for Objective #1

Objective #2 | Objective #2

Measures for Objective #2

Figure A.2 Goals, Objectives and Measures Worksheet Template.

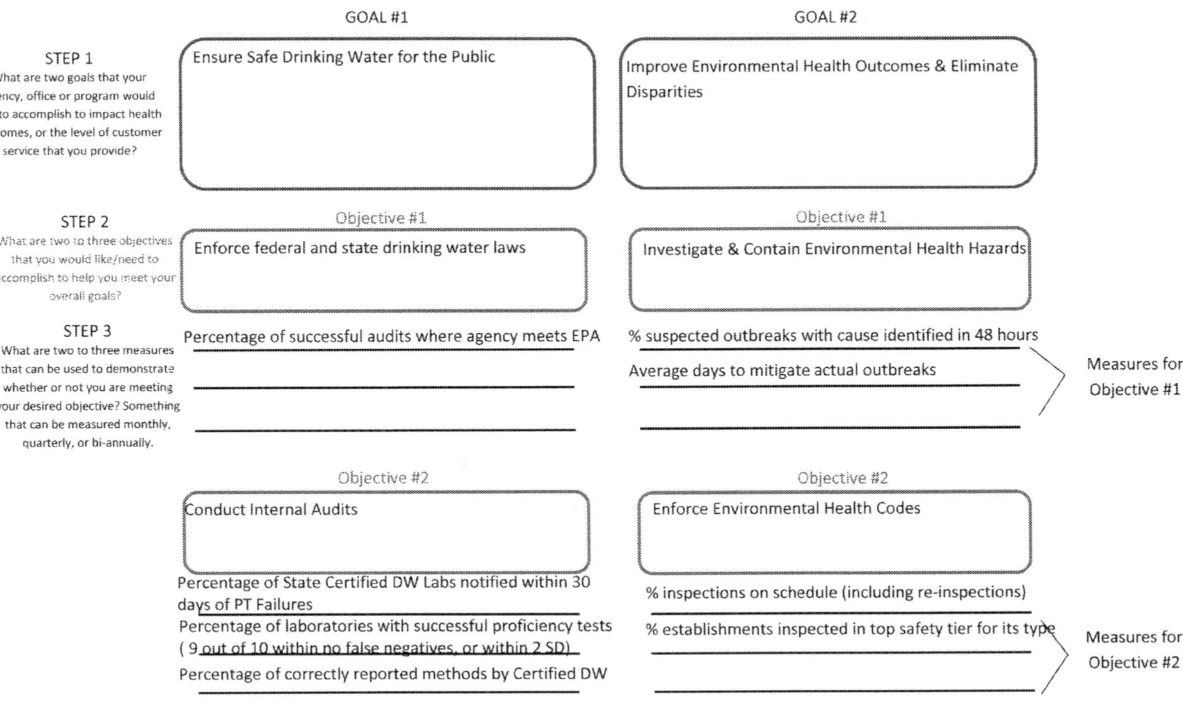

Figure A.3 Goals, Objectives and Measures Worksheet Template – Completed Example.

Public Health Performance Management Indicators						
Performance Measure	**Previous Period**	**Current Period**	**Target Current Period**	**Trend Direction**	**Number of Periods**	**Frequency**
COMMUNITY HEALTH OUTCOME Goals: Measures						
Percent of Medicaid women who smoke in the last three months of pregnancy		42%	39%	↑	1	Annually
Number of infant deaths due to SIDS/SUID		36	35	↑	1	Annually
Number of births to teenagers age 15-17		522	600	↓	1	Annually
Percent of third grade students with dental sealants		23%	32%	↓	1	Annually
COMMUNITY IMPLEMENTATION Objectives: Measures						
Number of women enrolled in quitline services	196	254	336	↑	4	Quarterly
Percentage of RFTS smoking clients enrolled in SCRIPT services		28%	35%	↓	1	Annually
Initiative: Develop a BPH communication plan for smoking during pregnancy		1	1	●	1	Annually
Number of WV Title I Elementary Schools with dental sealant programs	105	110	110	↑	4	Quarterly

Figure A.4 Example Performance Measures Dashboard.

Operating Plan Goals, Objectives, & Measures for:	State Health Department	Accreditation	Trend Direction					Support & Documentation	
	Objectives & Performance Measures								
Goal 1:	Objective or Activity: Enforce EH codes and laws	PHAB Domain	Previous Period	Current Period	Target	& No. Periods	Frequency	QI Plan	Notes
Improve EH outcomes and eliminate disparities	Measures:								
	% of eating estblishments inspected at least 1x every 12 months	6	72%	68%	100%	1	quarterly		
	% of eating establishments that pass inspection	1	96%	95%	95%	1	quarterly		
	# of eating establishments the fail re-inspection after first failure	2	0.00	0.00	3.00	2	quarterly		
	Objective or Activity: Investigate and contain EH hazards								
	Measures:								
	# of confirmed new food borne illnesses per quarter	2	2.00	3.00	3.00	1	quarterly		
	# of qualified homes given a home lead testing kits per quarter	3	173.00	100.00	80.00	2	quarterly		
	0	0							
	Objective or Activity: 0								
	Measures:								
	0	0							

Directional Key

Holding at or near previously reported values

Current Period is moving in desired direction

Current Period is moving opposite of desired direction

Figure A.5 PM Dashboard Example.

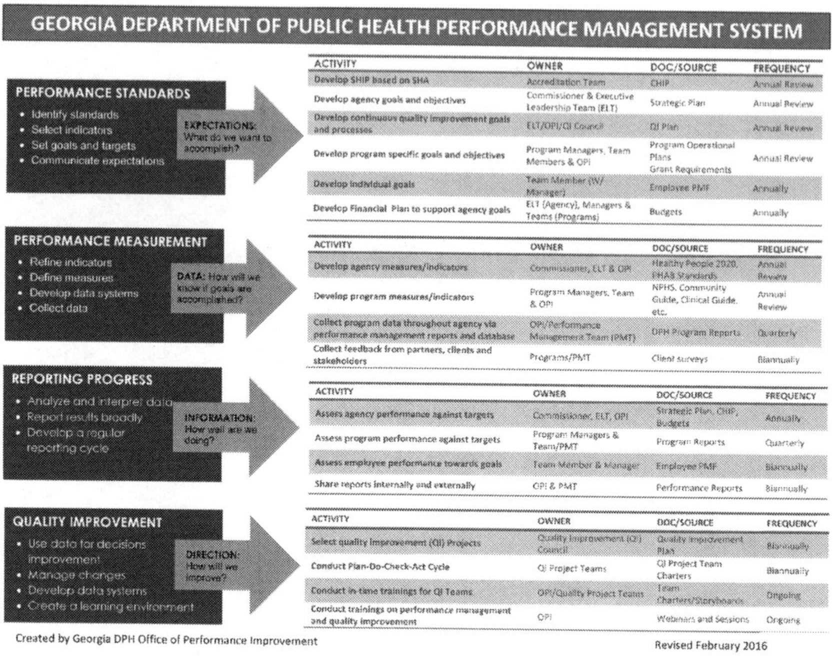

GEORGIA DEPARTMENT OF PUBLIC HEALTH PERFORMANCE MANAGEMENT SYSTEM

PERFORMANCE STANDARDS

- Identify standards
- Select indicators
- Set goals and targets
- Communicate expectations

EXPECTATIONS: What do we want to accomplish?

ACTIVITY	OWNER	DOC/SOURCE	FREQUENCY
Develop SHIP based on SHA	Accreditation Team	CHIP	Annual Review
Develop agency goals and objectives	Commissioner & Executive Leadership Team (ELT)	Strategic Plan	Annual Review
Develop continuous quality improvement goals and processes	ELT/OPI/QI Council	QI Plan	Annual Review
Develop program specific goals and objectives	Program Managers, Team Members & OPI	Program Operational Plans Grant Requirements	Annual Review
Develop individual goals	Team Member (W/ Manager)	Employee PMF	Annually
Develop Financial Plan to support agency goals	ELT (Agency), Managers & Teams (Programs)	Budgets	Annually

PERFORMANCE MEASUREMENT

- Refine indicators
- Define measures
- Develop data systems
- Collect data

DATA: How will we know if goals are accomplished?

ACTIVITY	OWNER	DOC/SOURCE	FREQUENCY
Develop agency measures/indicators	Commissioner, ELT & OPI	Healthy People 2020, PHAB Standards	Annual Review
Develop program measures/indicators	Program Managers, Team & OPI	NPHS, Community Guide, Clinical Guide, etc.	Annual Review
Collect program data throughout agency via performance management reports and database	OPI/Performance Management Team (PMT)	DPH Program Reports	Quarterly
Collect feedback from partners, clients and stakeholders	Programs/PMT	Client surveys	Biannually

REPORTING PROGRESS

- Analyze and interpret data
- Report results broadly
- Develop a regular reporting cycle

INFORMATION: How well are we doing?

ACTIVITY	OWNER	DOC/SOURCE	FREQUENCY
Assess agency performance against targets	Commissioner, ELT, OPI	Strategic Plan, CHIP, Budgets	Annually
Assess program performance against targets	Program Managers & Team/PMT	Program Reports	Quarterly
Assess employee performance towards goals	Team Member & Manager	Employee PMF	Biannually
Share reports internally and externally	OPI & PMT	Performance Reports	Biannually

QUALITY IMPROVEMENT

- Use data for decisions improvement
- Manage changes
- Develop data systems
- Create a learning environment

DIRECTION: How will we improve?

ACTIVITY	OWNER	DOC/SOURCE	FREQUENCY
Select quality improvement (QI) Projects	Quality Improvement (QI) Council	Quality Improvement Plan	Biannually
Conduct Plan-Do-Check-Act Cycle	QI Project Teams	QI Project Team Charters	Biannually
Conduct in-time trainings for QI Teams	OPI/Quality Project Teams	Team Charters/Storyboards	Ongoing
Conduct trainings on performance management and quality improvement	OPI	Webinars and Sessions	Ongoing

Created by Georgia DPH Office of Performance Improvement

Revised February 2016

Figure A.6 Georgia Department of Public Health PM System Outline.

Portsmouth Virginia Public Health Department

Smart Goal, Smarter Objective and Smartest Action Approach

The Portsmouth Virginia Public Health Department (PHD) uses a unique approach for setting a comprehensive set of SMART Goals and Smarter objectives related to each of their Strategic Priorities in their strategic plan as shown in Figure A.7.

Each PHD team uses their SWOTs and health and community data to expand on the goals and objectives to come up with Smartest Action to accomplish them.

Table A.1 shows the details of this unique approach to aligning the goals, objectives and actions in one comprehensive approach.

Developed by: Triona Gateley, Portsmouth Health Department, from the PHD 2014–2019 Strategic Plan.

Figure A.7 Portsmouth, Virginia Public Health Department – Smart Goal, Smarter Objective and Smartest Action.

Table A.1 Strategic Goals, Objectives and Actions Framework

Strategic Priority (Where we are directing our energy): 5 Years

Strategy (What we want to accomplish): 5 Years

Goal (How we are going to accomplish it) Organization Wide, Long-Term: 5 Years

S	Specific (and Strategic)	Specify what is to be achieved, by how much, and when; the goal should be well-defined and clear to anyone that has a basic knowledge of PHD what it is talking about
M	Measurable (and Meaningful)	Make sure that the goal can be measured
A	Achievable	Set goals that are feasible for the organization within the availability of resources, knowledge, and time; the goals should also be broad enough that they can be broken down into objectives for different levels within the organization to implement
R	Relevant	The goal should be relevant to our mission/vision/values and our Strategic Priorities
T	Time-oriented	Have a general timeframe for achieving the goal – have a year deadline

Objective (How we are going to measure progress) Department Level, Intermediate-Term: 3 Years

S	Specific	State exactly what you want to accomplish – who, what, where, when – the objectives should be more specific than the goals
M	Measurable	The objective should be measured in some way – this is how we show our progress toward the goal
A	Achievable	These objectives should be attainable, but should stretch and challenge our ability to achieve the outcome
R	Relevant	How is the objective aligned with the goal?
T	Time-oriented	The "by when" guide for your objective to successful and timely completion – have a month and year deadline
E	Actionable	Each objective should start with an action-oriented verb; then, when you read the objective in a year, you can remember what you wrote and you can do something about it
R	Responsible Person	Each objective needs a designated person who is in charge of seeing it get done (even if they are not directly carrying out the actions involved)

Action (What we will do to accomplish it) Team and Individual Level, Short-Term: 1–2 Years

S	Specific	Who, what, where, when, how – should be the most specific and look for more immediate actions
M	Measurable (and Manageable)	Have some measure to show how you've made progress toward the objective; break it into manageable chunks
A	Achievable	These actions should be attainable, but should stretch and challenge our ability to achieve the outcome
R	Relevant	Should be directly related to the objective
T	Time-oriented	Have specific and accountable deadlines
E	Assignable	Can give it to a specific person – have someone that does it
S	Simple	These are short-term actions, so should be smaller
T	Tangible	Getting into more specific actions

Index